The Hidden Valley Kings

I0129811

The Hidden Valley Kings

Series 1

<u>The Hidden Valley Kings</u>

Roscoe Abel

Published by Fountain of Life Publisher's House
P. O. Box 922612, Norcross, GA 30010
Phone: 404-936-3989 Website: www.pariceparker.biz
Please Email Manuscripts to: publish@pariceparker.biz

Fountain of Life Publishing House is committed to excellence in the publishing industry. The Company reflects the philosophy established by the founder, based on Psalm 68:11, *"The Lord gave the word and great was the company of those who published it."*

Cover Design by Tasha Kinney
Editor: F. O. L. P. H. Authored by: Roscoe Abell

Published in the United States of America
Copyright Library of Congress
ISBN: 978 -1-956924-05-3
Date: August 8, 2022

DEDICATION

To all the young black children living in poverty,
my Hidden Valley family and all that's incarcerated.

Roscoe Abell

The Hidden Valley Kings

CONTENTS

The Hidden Valley Kings

Introduction

This book is part of a series that gives you a look into the life of Roscoe Abel in the Hidden Valley Kings. Roscoe was one of the founders of the Hidden Valley Kings out of Charlotte, North Carolina. The Hidden Valley Kings was the first most lethal gang that originated in Hidden Valley of Charlotte, NC. The (HVK) Hidden Valley Kings was featured on an episode of the hit TV series gangland also; Roscoe was featured in an urban magazine called as is Roscoe Abell; while in prison transformed from having a criminal mentality and turning it into a revolutionary psyche Roscoe Abell is now the Assistant chairman for the WL Nolan mentorship program which was started in 2012 this program is designed to help the black community to understand why they are oppressed and how to combat oppression Roscoe is. Also, an advocate for assisting political prisoners, he is now a member of the new African revolutionary nationalist. Others have tried to tell you, his story. However, the true story has not been told until now. Hear about the streets of Hidden Valley from one of their own, a legend in his own right Mr. Roscoe Abel the original King.

Roscoe Abell

Chapter 1

Wilmore Drive

I was born in Charlotte North Carolina at Carolina medical center both my sisters was also born at Carolina medical center me and my sisters are originally from the Willmore community my mom and dad are originally from South Carolina and moved to Charlotte looking for a better life my dad worked odd jobs from time to time but that wasn't enough money to make ends meet so he ended up dabbling in the street affairs this was when I was introduced to the gangster life because my father took me everywhere he went. It was during these times that I met guys like Ned Johnson, Redman June, Detroit Fred, Mook and Clyde Potlow, Sonny Funderburk, Miss Angela and so many hustlers, gangsters, and prostitutes that is too many for me to name at this time. If I remember correctly our address was 314 merman avenue we lived in a white duplex and next door there was a liquor house attached. My father took me in that liquor house plenty of times when I was a kid. There was another liquor house on Wilmore Street, and it was at this liquor house that I observed everything go down. The liquor house on Wilmore Street brings back many memories. I remember a time when an older guy who was I was born in Charlotte North Carolina at Carolina medical center both my sisters was also born at Carolina medical center me and my sisters are originally from the Willmore community my mom and dad are originally from South Carolina and moved to Charlotte looking for a better life my dad worked odd jobs from time to time but that wasn't enough money to make ends meet so he ended up dabbling in the street affairs this was when I was introduced to the gangster life because my father took me everywhere he went. It was during these times that I met guys like Ned Johnson, Redman June, Detroit Fred, Mook and Clyde Potlow, Sonny Funderburk, Miss Angela and so many hustlers', gangsters and prostitutes that is too many for me to name at this time. If I remember correctly our address was 314 Merman Avenue we lived in a white duplex and next door there was a liquor house attached. My father took me in that liquor house plenty of times when I was a kid.

There was another liquor house on Wilmore Street, and it was at this liquor house that I watched everything go down. The liquor house on Wilmore Street brings back many memories. I remember a time when an older guy who was pretty much drunk kept bothering me and being very disrespectful in the things he said about my father. After a few minutes I became very upset and kicked the man in his shin because my father was my hero, and I would not let anyone talk anything bad about my father. The man then grab me by the back of my head and threw me to the ground at that time a young pretty lady who named I can't recall ran into the liquor house and got my father my father ran out the liquor house straight over to the man hitting him over the head with a 38 snub nose. As the man fell to the ground my dad pistol whips him repeatedly. The lady who had ran and got my father grab me by the hand and led me into the liquor house. I can hear a lot of commotion going on outside and that was the first time I had ever seen my father react in such a violent manner with a gun. But it damn sure wasn't the last time. The Wilmore community was a low-income poverty striking community where a lot of people was very poor but was rich in spirit and love. As a child I always look forward to Wilmore Day which was a day of celebration that brought the community together with festivities. I always had a ball it was like an amusement park to a child. Everyone was dressed in their Sunday's best. Also around this time you had several different gangs some of them I remember was the He-Man and G-Man and these two groups always clash at Queens Park movie theater there were other gangs that came a couple years later like the "Mustang gang", the "Kango gang", the Playboys, the BDP and others scattered around the city of Charlotte as a youngster I always claim the G-Man but was really too young to be an actual member I remember taking a switchblade to Eastover elementary School and pulling it out on a guy after he stole my pencil and I told him I was a G-Man and that I would stab him the guy told on me and I was sent to the principal office a letter was sent home to my mother in which she beat the daylights out of me. I always wanted to be like my father, so I mimicked everything he did. You see I became traumatized by my environment because my father kept me with him as much as possible and by my father being a hustler, I was privileged to see The gangster lifestyle up close and personal. My father was a very violent man and I believe I took on his characteristics over the years. My father also had a heart of gold that was pure towards the ones he loved friends and family alike. But he had a mean streak that if once crossed there was no turning back. I remember one day walking down Wilmore Street with a prostitute by the name of Lodi Potlow whom I called auntie when a man pulled up and jumped out the car and snatched her by her hair and slung her to the ground and started kicking her, she screamed out to me and told me to run but instead I stood there in shock unable to move. As the man continue to stump her, I came to my senses and ran over to the guy and bit down real hard on his thigh the man backhanded me, and I fell to the ground with a busted lip. At this time auntie ran over to me and grab me trying to shield me from the guy but the guy grabbed her by her hair once again and continued to beat her we were only a few houses down from the liquor house where my father was at, so I ran back to the liquor house and told my father and when he seen my busted lip, he took off running and at this time a lady grabs me and sat me between her legs and covered my ears. I didn't understand why she was covering my ears after a few moments my father ran back into the house with blood on his shirt and asked where his son was at. It was then he asked Redman June to take me home to my mother we only live one street over I can remember a few moments later hearing sirens. My father didn't get in till later that night, but he had company with him and being the nosy child, I was I crept to the end of the hallway to listen. I heard a voice say we got rid of the gun so you should be good. I didn't really know what they meant by that statement until I got older and that's when I knew my father had killed the man. My father was a hustler, but he was more of a shooter for my godfather named Ned Johnson I don't remember too much about my godfather except that he always gave me and his son money to go play video games at the Big Apple store. His son and I were very close I can't recall his name, but I did learn that he committed suicide years later. It was said that my godfather could not count but he had so much money that it really didn't matter. If one was to look at him, you wouldn't believe he was as rich as he was because he always dressed down in a painter's suit. There was a time in the 80s when it was a drug war in the Wilmore community, I really don't know all the details since I was only a kid about 7 years old, but I do remember my father being in that war. I don't know what caused this war nor do I know all the people involved but I do remember someone trying to assassinate my father one day while we was on

The Hidden Valley Kings

Kinston avenue in the Wilmore community if my memory served correctly it was about around high noon and I believe me and my father was on our way to a softball game and I remember us stopping at the stop sign on the corner of Kingston and South Tryon when a car pulled up and started shooting at my father. My father yelled for me to get down and push my head down to the floor mat I remember my father driving in reverse shooting out the driver side window I don't know what happened after that, but I do know the shooting stopped and when I looked up, we were crossing over headed towards the Big Apple store. My father made me go into the store the owner of the store was good friends with my father. I don't remember how long I remained in that store, but I do remember playing video games all day because the big Apple store had a game room right next to it. There were kids ranging from the ages of six or seven into their late teens that love coming to that game room. That was the spot. I don't remember how I got home that evening, but I do remember going home and my mother crying. The next morning is when I found out that my father was wanted for murder. He ran to my auntie's house in New York City. A few months later my father was captured in New York and sent to Rikers island it was rumored that one of our relatives had turned him in. My mother took me and my sister with her to New York to my auntie's house so that we can go visit our father at Rikers island I don't remember much about that place, but I do remember having to take a bus and I also

13

remember going through a turntable to get in the building. After a couple of months my father was extradited back to Charlotte North Carolina to face trial after about a good 8 months the charge was dismissed.

However, it wouldn't be long before my father was arrested again and sent to State prison. While my father was away my mother experienced hardships, but she still kept the family together and begin to work odd jobs to keep food on the table and clothes on our backs.

Chapter 2

Dark Skin Lady

I remember as a child a lady whose name I don't recall used to leave letters or notes on our door threatening my mother saying that she was going to kill her as soon as she caught up with her this lady claimed that my mother testified against her in court on a murder charge which sent the lady away for a long time. One time I remember late at night someone grabbed our doorknob and began shaking the door as if they were trying to get in my mom asked who was at the door but never received a response my mother then went into the back room and grabbed my father shotgun and began shooting through the door, I heard a loud yep which indicated whoever was on the other side of the door had been hit and whoever they were left. A couple of weeks later my father was released from prison. One night while my mother was cooking my father had the front door wide open and a dark skin lady approached the door my father asked if he could help her, and the lady said she was looking for someone named Dot which is my mother's name my mother then came to the door and my father asked my mom if he knew the

15

lady in which my mom responded no and the lady then said you are not the Dot that I'm looking for. Come to find out it was the lady who had been leaving the letters and notes threatening my mother. She apologized saying that a lady by the name of Dot had lived there years ago before she had gone to prison and that she had testified against her she apologized to my mother and we never seen or heard from her again. My mom is a sweet lady but can be devious if pushed too far. She stayed in a lot of fights with other women behind my father and have even went to jail a couple times. My mom had a heart of gold and she loved her kids very much and she would do anything to make sure we were taken care of I've seen my mom lie cheat still just to have food on the table when my dad was incarcerated. When my father began to get hooked on his own supply things got worse and everything went downhill from there. There were many nights that we did not have food on the table which led my mom to take drastic measures to make sure her kids were fed. Coming up I didn't have the luxury of being able to wear Jordan sneakers or Polo outfits or Nikes for that matter my mom always bought me what we called back in the day jeepers shoes that didn't have a name to them I've went weeks without a haircut however my mom did what she could in order for me and my sisters to have a roof over my head clean clothes on our backs. Around 1985 we finally moved out of the Wilmore community and move to a neighborhood called Hidden Valley on the north side of Charlotte it was here when my life began to change. When we first move into the Hidden Valley community, we thought we had struck big I was definitely excited when I learned that there was a movie theater only walking distance from my house. The neighborhood was so big that I used to always get lost my first few months moving there. It took me a while to learn myself around this big neighborhood I always got lost especially at nighttime. I remember getting into multiple fights because I was the new kid on the block and my clothes were ragged. however, I did become great friends with the same guys that I fought every day. As a young child I remember there were lots of activity going on down the street from my house this area was called Beachway Apartments and Caesars Ford I lived on Wellingford Street. Welling Ford Street Beachway and Caesars Ford Apartments is where everything was going down at. I used to walk down the street to the park which really wasn't a park all they had was a basketball goal, but everyone used to hang out at this court. It was always large crowds especially in the summertime and I used to go down there and watch the older guys play basketball. There were a lot of girls and women hanging around also I remember one day going to the basketball court as the new guy I was beaten up on by an older guy. I took off running back to the house while everyone was laughing, I went into the backyard and grabbed my aluminum bat. I got back to the court with the bat in my hand I heard one of the girls say uh-oh hear that boy come back. The guy who had beat me up wasn't paying attention as he was still playing basketball, I ran up on him and swung with all my might towards his kneecaps he collapsed to the pavement as I continue to beat him over and over again until one of the girls grabbed me and told me everything was going to be okay it was only then I began to calm down with tears running down my face. The guy was so f***** up he could not move in fact they had to call an ambulance I don't remember the girl's name, but I always remembered her chocolate face and loop earrings and puma shoes and all white mini skirt. At that time, I believe I was 11 years old and was already a custom to violence. I remember my first day of school at hidden valley elementary I was in the second grade and felt like the kids that was there was completely different than my friends from the Wilmore community. I stayed in many fights at hidden valley elementary School many people thought I was just a bad kid but I was a new kid in the neighborhood so I had to prove myself at first I really didn't like fighting but after a while I began loving it and was in a fight almost every day at least three to four times a week it got to a point that I began fighting guys that were a lot older than me since there wasn't many in my age bracket that could out throw them hands with me. I used to walk from one end of hidden valley to the other side fighting any and whoever wanted to come out in the street and throw them hands. It was a lot of fun for me I went home plenty of nights with busted lips and I sent many homes with black eyes and busted Jaws

The Hidden Valley Kings

I stayed in trouble throughout hidden valley elementary School it was the fifth grade I believe when I first really started trying to sell dope I f***** up many packs as a kid and was always running from the older guys who carried guns looking for me cousin I f***** up their money. It wasn't hard to f*** the money up considering I was a kid I usually was taking advantage of by the grown crackheads that was more Street smart than I was and other times I spent money on just buying lots of pizza for my friends or paying everyone's way into the movies I was never really materialistic, so I never even bothered to buy

clothes or shoes plus the older guys never gave me no more than a 300 pack back then and I was only getting 20 off a hundred this was in the '80s sometime around the early '90s I was getting 40 off of 100 even then I was still f****** up n***** packs I was never truly a hustler not when it came to selling dope I took many losses and I always felt the money that I didn't lose by someone gaming me or finessing me out of it was mine like for instance if I had a $300 pack and only $100 of it was mine, if I was tricked out of at least $200 then I just kept $100 for myself not thinking about the person I owed cousin I always felt I had to get something s*** I've been out here all day and it ain't my fault they took advantage of me I was a kid but I had enough sense to know as a kid that I was going to get something out of it. Sometime around the second grade I begin doing backflips and became one of the best throughout my neighborhood there were a lot of back flippers.

The Hidden Valley Kings

Back then no one in my age group could out flip me so I used to challenge guys that were a couple grades higher than me or in junior high school I even challenge grown men but I always lost because my little legs wasn't yet developed which only made me practice even harder to do the impossible which was to beat the guys that were a lot older than me so I decided to do something that no one had ever did in hidden valley history at that time not that I know of and that was a double tuck backflip off the school building I didn't intend to do a double tap I just forgot to untuck and as I stay balled up I continue to rotate and landed on my feet that flip there went into the hidden valley history books and another thing I had did was did backflips all the way across hidden valley elementary School field this was before they put the octopus up which was a big mound of dirt with about 6 to 8 arms coming out of it. When was first built all the guys used to go to the top and play King of the Hill that got boring and died out quickly, so we began using the arms as ramps to jump? Everyone had bikes in hidden valley back in those days and we used to ride in packs back then it was a lot different than what it is today I remember running around the neighborhood snatching apples and plums in people front and backyards we always had a lookout why everyone else went and raided the trees those were the fun days. now if you run in somebody yard you will be shot. There wasn't a lot of violence back then however there were lots of fights. There were only a couple shooters back then.

Chapter 3

Big Time Hustler

Hidden valley was always known where the pretty boys and pretty girls resided at and it also had a reputation where all the dope boys were from there was hustlers all over the city of Charlotte, but hidden valley was rumored to be the plug of Charlotte. There were a few big-Time hustlers back in those days in hidden valley, but I would not name them because they are still living. Even had a few women. I began trying to sell drugs around the year of 88 but I was never good at it, it was just something to do really. I was more of a troublemaker because that lifestyle was exciting it gave me an adrenaline rush. I was cool with a lot of people growing up but around 87 I became best friends with a guy named Ready he had an older brother named Roland me and Ready became close at a very young age and I remember we used to go to the Ecker's drug store and steal all the candy and Snicker bars. Ready was a hustler at a very young age all the merchandise we stole out of Eckerd he used to sell it at Hidden Valley Elementary School, and I used to give mine away to the girls. I just never really cared about money it wasn't something I was excited about. But I was excited about building up a name. And that's why I always stayed in s*** I also had a reputation as being a tender dick this means I fell in love easily and I was always faithful to any girl I was dating I've never cheated on any girl in my life and my friends used to tease me about this. I really didn't care though it was a wonderful feeling to be in love the only thing I probably love more than a female was getting the adrenaline rush from getting in trouble. Me and my best friend Ready was opposite as night and day he was the smooth pretty boy and nice dresser, and I was the aggressive thuggish dresser but yet and still we had mad love for each other, and I was willing to die or even kill to make sure he was safe. I actually met Ready older brother Roland first on the basketball court in Caesars Ford apartments. It was on a hot summer day when I got into a fight with two guys on the basketball court although I was losing the battle, I never gave up I fought so hard that the guys I was fighting said the hell with it and begin running I had too much energy and too much heart.

Roland walked over to me and said I like the way you held your own I want to introduce you to my little brother I followed Roland back to their apartment in Caesars Ford and that's when he introduced me to his younger brother Ready. Ready had this Superior aura about himself as if everyone was beneath him I didn't like him because I thought he felt he was better than me but I later learn it wasn't any of that he just had confidence in himself and was a born leader after going up to the apartment everyday me and ready became closer and closer and I began to spend the night over there house during the weekends to best describe our friendship he was Cane and I was O dog in the movie menace to society. Me and Ready became closer than friends we became Brothers. Sometime around 1992 we Begin stealing cars together. I actually began stealing cars before that with another group of friends in the year 1990. Along with me and Ready there was about six of us and we just joy ride around the neighborhood looking for outsiders who came through the neighborhood. In the Summer of 1992 me and Ready was sitting in a stolen car in Beech Way apartments inside the hidden valley community listening to the rapper Scar Face. As I was pulling from my Newport cigarette. I heard what sounded like gunshots I looked at ready and said man did you hear that and Ready replied did I hear what? I turned the radio down and cocked my head to the side to hear better. I heard the shots again and this time so did Ready. At that point I was already opening the passenger door jumping out the car with my 38 in my hand. Cover me I said to Ready as I begin running up the hill in Beech Way apartments towards the gunshots. It had been cloudy all that day and it had just started to drizzle as I was running up the hill heading towards Caesars Ford apartments which was located right beside Beech Way. As I made it to the end of Caesars Ford apartments, I peeked my head around the apartment building at that moment I heard a loud boom which scared the s*** out of me and I jump back with my heart racing. What the f*** you scared of I heard Ready say as he ran up behind me it's only thunder n****I looked up at the sky and seen the clouds getting darker and darker. Within that split second we heard more gunshots. I looked around apartment building once again and seen two dark skin n***** shooting at my partner Kool-Aid.

Kool-Aid was ducked behind a white Cherokee and every second he'll pop up and let off a round or two. I ran out from side of the apartments with my 38 in hand and let off three shots as I ran towards the dumpster for cover. Ready stayed on the side of the apartment complex as he begins shooting at the dark skin n***** as well. I peeked around the dumpster and let off two more shots in the direction of one tall dark skin n****I heard Kool-Aid yell out that he was out of bullets I yelled back to him and told him that I was going to run towards him, and I asked Ready to cover me as I ran towards Kool-Aid. I let off one more shot and duck beside the Cherokee with my n****I can hear bullets penetrating the Cherokee that we were hiding behind I crawled on my belly towards the back end of the Cherokee and picked around the tire as I aim to pull the trigger, but nothing came out that's when I knew my chamber was empty damn, I said to Kool-Aid I'm out of bullets. I look back at Kool-Aid and realize he had been shot. I lean my back up against the back tire of the

Cherokee as I dump the shells put them in my pocket and begin reloading my 38. as I put the last bullet into the chamber, I heard screeching tires that's when I looked up and seen a green Buick speeding out of Caesars Ford apartments I ran towards the Buick and squeezed off three shots Ready yelled to me that he was going to go and get the car and that he would be right back. I could hear sirens at a distance as I ran towards Kool-Aid to help my n**** up I threw Kool-Aid around my neck as I begin to half drag and half carry him across the parking lot. Ready pulled up and helped me put Kool-Aid in the backseat. As we begin speeding out of Caesars Ford two or three police cars was coming towards us. Ready slowed down to not bring attention to us but the police cars turn right around and begin giving Chase. Ready smashed the gas speeding towards Sugar Creek Road. We made a short left on to Sugar Creek Road almost hitting another car. We continued down Sugar Creek running a red light crossing over North Tryon Street. By the time we got to the Plaza extension the rain was coming down heavy. We crossed over the Plaza heading towards East way drive. Once we reached East way Ready made a sharp right turn which caused the car to spin around hitting another car. At that moment I was already jumping out the car running. I was finally captured on Grainger high school campus. I was handcuffed and dragged into the back seat of the police car. Yep, y'all boys really outdid yourself this time the police said as we were headed towards the station. Yep, you really f***** up. He continued and on about how we going to do life in prison. I zoned out looking up at the dark clouds as the rain continued to fall. I was concerned about my partner Kool Aid knowing that he had been shot. I began thinking about everything that led up to my life at that point. All the fights all the shootouts and all the stress. Damn! Is this the way I'm going to be for the rest of my life I remember thinking to myself? it wasn't long before we reached the police station was pretty much drunk kept bothering me and being very disrespectful in the things he said about my father. After a few minutes I became very upset and kicked the man in his shin because my father was my hero, and I would not let anyone talk anything bad about my father. The man then grabs me by the back of my head and threw me to the ground at that time a young pretty lady who named I can't recall ran into the liquor house and got my father my father ran out the liquor house straight over to the man hitting him over the head with a 38-snub nose. As the man fell to the ground my dad pistol whipped him repeatedly. The lady who had ran and got my father grab me by the hand and led me into the liquor house. I can hear a lot of commotion going on outside that was the first time I ever seen my father react in such a violent manner with a gun and it damn sure wasn't the last time. The Wilmore community was a low-income poverty striking community where a lot of people was very poor but was rich in spirit and love. As a child I always look forward to Wilmore Day which was a day of celebration that brought the community together with festivities. I always had a ball it was like an amusement park to a child. Everyone was dressed in their Sunday's best. Also around this time you had several different gangs some of them I remember was the He-Man and G-Man and these two groups always clash at Queens Park movie theater there were other gangs that came a couple years later like the mustang gang, the kango gang, the Playboys, the BDP and others scattered around the city of Charlotte as a youngster I always claim the G-Man but was really too young to be an actual member I remember taking a switchblade to Eastover elementary School and pulling it out on a guy after he stole my pencil and I told him I was a G-Man and that I would stab him the guy told on me and I was sent to the principal office a letter was sent home to my mother in which she beat the daylights out of me.

Chapter 4

The Gangster Lifestyle

I always wanted to be like my father, so I mimicked everything he did. You see I became traumatized by my environment because my father kept me with him as much as possible and by my father being a hustler, I was privileged to see the "gangster" lifestyle up close and personal. My father was a very violent man and I believe I took on his characteristics over the years. My father also had a heart of gold that was pure towards the ones he loved friends and family alike. But he had a mean streak that if once crossed there was no turning back. I remember one day walking down Wilmore Street with a prostitute by the name of Lodi Potlow whom I called auntie when a man pulled up and jumped out the car and snatched her by her hair and slung her to the ground and started kicking her, she screamed out to me and told me to run but instead I stood there in shock unable to move. As the man continue to stump her, I came to my senses and ran over to the guy and bit down real hard on his thigh the man backhanded me, and I fell to the ground with a busted lip. At this time auntie ran over to me and grab me trying to shield me from the guy but the guy grabbed her by her hair once again and continued to beat her we were only a few houses down from the liquor house where my father was at, so I ran back to the liquor house and told my father and when he seen my busted lip, he took off running and at this time a lady grabs me and sat me between her legs and covered my ears. I didn't understand why she was covering my ears after a few moments my father ran back into the house with blood on his shirt and asked where his son was at. It was then he asked Redman June to take me home to my mother we only live one street over I can remember a few moments later hearing sirens. My father didn't get in till later that night, but he had company with him and being the nosy child, I was I crept to the end of the hallway to listen. I heard a voice say we got rid of the gun so you should be good. I didn't really know what they meant by that statement until I got older and that's when I knew my father had killed the man. My father was a hustler, but he was more of a shooter for my godfather named Ned Johnson I don't remember too much about my godfather except that he always gave me and his son money to go play video games at the Big Apple store. His son and I were very close I can't recall his name, but I did learn that he committed suicide years later. It was said that my godfather could not count but he had so much money that it really didn't matter. If one was to look at him, you wouldn't believe he was as rich as he was because he always dressed down in a painter's suit. There

The Hidden Valley Kings

was a time in the 80s when it was a drug war in the Wilmore community, I really don't know all the details since I was only a kid about 7 years old, but I do remember my father being in that war. I don't know what caused this war nor do I know all the people involved but I do remember someone trying to assassinate my father one day while we was on Kinston avenue in the Wilmore community if my memory served correctly it was about around high noon and I believe me and my father was on our way to a softball game and I remember us stopping at the stop sign on the corner of Kingston and South Tryon when a car pulled up and started shooting at my father. My father yelled for me to get down and push my head down to the floor mat I remember my father driving in reverse shooting out the driver side window I don't know what happened after that, but I do know the shooting stopped and when I looked up, we were crossing over headed towards the Big Apple store. My father made me go into the store the owner of the store was good friends with my father. I don't remember how long I remained in that store, but I do remember playing video games all day because the big Apple store had a game room right next to it. There were kids ranging from the ages of six or seven into their late teens that love coming to that game room. That was the spot. I don't remember how I got home that evening, but I do remember going home and my mother crying. The next morning is when I found out that my father was wanted for murder. He ran to my auntie's house in New York City. A few months later my father was captured in New York and sent to Rikers island it was rumored that one of our relatives had turned him in. My mother took me and my sister with her to New York to my auntie's house so that we can go visit our father at Rikers island I don't remember much about that place, but I do remember having to take a bus and I also remember going through a turntable to get in the building. After a couple of months my father was extradited back to Charlotte North Carolina to face trial after about a good 8 months the charge was dismissed. However, it wouldn't be long before my father was arrested again and sent to State prison. While my father was away my mother experienced hardships, but she kept the family together and begin to work odd jobs to keep food on the table and clothes on our backs. I remember as a child a lady whose name I don't recall used to leave letters or notes on our door threatening my mother saying that she was going to kill her as soon as she caught up with her this lady claimed that my mother testified against her in court on a murder charge which sent the lady away for a long time. One time I remember late at night someone grabbed our doorknob and began shaking the door as if they were trying to get in my mom asked who was at the door but never received a response my mother then went into the back room and grabbed my father shotgun and began shooting through the door, I heard a loud yep which indicated whoever was on the other side of the door had been hit and whoever they were left. A couple of weeks later my father was released from prison. One night while my mother was cooking my father had the front door wide open and a dark skin lady approached the door my father asked if he could help her, and the lady said she was looking for someone named Dot which is my mother's name my mother then came to the door and my father asked my mom if he knew the lady in which my mom responded no and the lady then said you are not the Dot that I'm looking for. Come to find out it was the lady who had been leaving the letters and notes threatening my mother. She apologized saying that a lady by the name of Dot had lived there years ago before she had gone to prison and that she had testified against her she apologized to my mother, and we never seen or heard from her again. My mom is a sweet lady but can be devious if pushed too far. She stayed in a lot of fights with other women behind my father and have even went to jail a couple times. My mom had a heart of gold, and she loved her kids very much and she would do anything to make sure we were taken care of I've seen my mom lie cheat still just to have food on the table when my dad was incarcerated. When my father began to get hooked on his own supply things got worse and everything went downhill from there. There were many nights that we did not have food on the table which led my mom to take drastic measures to make sure her kids were fed. Coming up I didn't have the luxury of being able to wear Jordan or Polo outfits or Nikes for that matter my mom always bought me what we called back in the day jeepers shoes that didn't have a name to them I've went weeks without a haircut however my mom did what she could in order for me and my sisters to have a roof over my head clean clothes on our backs. Around 1985 we finally moved out of the Wilmore community and move to a neighborhood called Hidden Valley on the north side of Charlotte it was here when my life began to change. When we first move into the Hidden Valley community, we thought we had struck big I was definitely excited when I learned that there was a movie theater only walking distance from my house. The neighborhood was so big that I used to always get lost my first few months moving there. It took me a while to learn myself around this big neighborhood I always got lost especially at nighttime. I remember getting into multiple fights because I was the new kid on the block and my clothes were ragged. However, I did become great friends with the same guys that I fought every day. As a young child I remember there were lots of activity going on down the street from my house this area was called Beachway apartments, and Caesars Ford I lived on Wellingford Street. Welling Ford Street Beachway and Caesars Ford apartments is where everything was going down at. I used to walk down the street to the park which really wasn't a park all they had was a basketball goal, but everyone used to hang out at this court. It was always large crowds especially in the summertime and I used to go down there and watch the older guys play basketball. There were a lot of girls and women hanging around also I

remember one day going to the basketball court as the new guy I was beaten up on by an older guy. I took off running back to the house while everyone was laughing, I went into the backyard and grabbed my aluminum bat. I got back to the court with the bat in my hand I heard one of the girls say uh-oh hear that boy come back. The guy who had beat me up wasn't paying attention as he was still playing basketball, I ran up on him and swung with all my might towards his kneecaps he collapsed to the pavement as I continue to beat him over and over again until one of the girls grabbed me and told me everything was going to be okay it was only then I began to calm down with tears running down my face. The guy was so f***** up he could not move in fact they had to call an ambulance I don't remember the girl's name, but I always remembered her chocolate face and loop earrings and puma shoes and all white mini skirt. At that time, I believe I was 11 years old and was already a custom to violence. I remember my first day of school at hidden valley elementary I was in the second grade and felt like the kids that was there was completely different than my friends from the Wilmore community. I stayed in many fights at hidden valley elementary School many people thought I was just a bad kid but I was a new kid in the neighborhood so I had to prove myself at first I really didn't like fighting but after a while I began loving it and was in a fight almost every day at least three to four times a week it got to a point that I began fighting guys that were a lot older than me since there wasn't many in my age bracket that could out throw them hands with me. I used to walk from one end of hidden valley to the other side fighting any and whoever wanted to come out in the street and throw them hands. It was a lot of fun for me I went home plenty of nights with busted lips and I sent many home with black eyes and busted Jaws I stayed in trouble throughout hidden valley elementary School it was the fifth grade I believe when I first really started trying to sell dope I f***** up many packs as a kid and was always running from the older guys who carried guns looking for me because I f***** up their money. It wasn't hard to f*** the money up considering I was a kid I usually was taking advantage of by the grown crackheads that was more Street smart than I was and other times I spent money on just buying lots of pizza for my friends or paying everyone's way into the movies I was never really materialistic so I never even bothered to buy clothes or shoes plus the older guys never gave me no more than a 300 pack back then and I was only getting 20 off a hundred this was in the '80s sometime around the early '90s I was getting 40 off of 100 even then I was still f****** up n***** packs I was never truly a hustler not when it came to selling dope I took many losses and I always felt the money that I didn't lose by someone gaming me or finessing me out of it was mine like for instance if I had a $300 pack and only $100 of it was mine, if I was tricked out of at least $200 then I just kept $100 for myself not thinking about the person I owed because I always felt I had to get something s*** I've been out here all day ain't my fault they took advantage of me I was a kid but I had enough sense to know as a kid that I was going to get something out of it. Sometime around the second grade I begin doing backflips and became one of the best throughout my neighborhood there were a lot of back flippers back then no one in my age group could out flip me so I used to challenge guys that were a couple grades higher than me or in junior high school I even challenge grown men but I always lost because my little legs wasn't yet developed which only made me practice even harder to do the impossible which was to beat the guys that were a lot older than me so I decided to do something that no one had ever did in hidden valley history at that time not that I know of and that was a double tuck backflip off the school building I didn't intend to do a double tap I just forgot to untuck and as I stay balled up I continue to rotate and landed on my feet that flip there went into the hidden valley history books and another thing I had did was did backflips all the way across hidden valley elementary School field this was before they put the octopus up which was a big mound of dirt with about 6 to 8 arms coming out of it. When was first built all the guys used to go to the top and play King of the Hill that got boring and died out quickly, so we began using the arms as ramps to jump? Everyone had bikes in hidden valley back in those days and we used to ride in packs back then it was a lot different than what it is today I remember running around the neighborhood snatching apples and plums in people front and backyards we always had a lookout why everyone else went and raided the trees those were the fun days. now if you run in somebody yard you will be shot. There wasn't a lot of violence back then however there were lots of fights there were only a couple shooters back then.

Hidden valley was always known where the pretty boys and pretty girls resided at and it also

had a reputation where all the dope boys were from there was hustlers all over the city of Charlotte, but hidden valley was rumored to be the plug of Charlotte. There were a few big Time

hustlers back in those days in hidden valley but I would not name them because they are still living. Even had a few women.

Chapter 5

The Loud Boom

I began trying to sell drugs around the year of 88 but I was never good at it, it was just something to do really. I was more of a troublemaker because that lifestyle was exciting it gave me an adrenaline rush. I was cool with a lot of people growing up but around 87 I became best friends with a guy named Ready he had an older brother named Roland me and Ready became close at a very young age and I remember we used to go to the Ecker's drug store and steal all the candy and Snicker bars. Ready was a hustler at a very young age all the merchandise we stole out of Eckerd he used to sell it at hidden valley elementary School, and I used to give mine away to the girls. I just never really cared about money it wasn't something I was excited about. But I was excited about building up a name. And that's why I always stayed in s*** I also had a reputation as being a tender dick this means I fell in love easily and I was always faithful to any girl I was dating I've never cheated on any girl in my life and my friends used to tease me about this. I really didn't care though it was a wonderful feeling to be in love the only thing I probably love more than a female was getting the adrenaline rush from getting in trouble. Me and my best friend Ready was opposite as night and day he was the smooth pretty boy and nice dresser, and I was the aggressive thuggish dresser but yet and still we had mad love for each other, and I was willing to die or even kill to make sure he was safe. I actually met Ready older brother Roland first on the basketball court in Caesars Ford apartments. It was on a hot summer day when I got into a fight with two guys on the basketball court although I was losing the battle, I never gave up I fought so hard that the guys I was fighting said the hell with it and begin running I had too much energy and too much heart.

Roland walked over to me and said I like the way you held your own I want to introduce you to my little brother I followed Roland back to their apartment in Caesars Ford and that's when he introduced me to his younger brother Ready. Ready had this Superior aura about himself as if everyone was beneath him I didn't like him because I thought he felt he was better than me but I later learn it wasn't any of that he just had confidence in himself and was a born leader after going up to the apartment everyday me and ready became closer and closer and I began to spend the night over there house during the weekends to best describe our friendship he was Cane and I was O dog in the movie menace to society. Me and Ready became closer than friends we became Brothers. Sometime around 1992 we Begin stealing cars together. I actually began stealing cars before that with another group of friends in the year 1990. Along with me and Ready there was about six of us and we just joy ride around the neighborhood looking for outsiders who came through the neighborhood. In the Summer of 1992 me and Ready was sitting in a stolen car in Beech Way apartments inside the hidden valley community listening to the rapper Scar Face. As I was pulling from my Newport cigarette, I heard what sounded like gunshots I looked at ready and said man did you hear that and Ready replied did I hear what? I turned the radio down and cocked my head to the side to hear better. I heard the shots again and this time so did Ready. At that point I was already opening the passenger door jumping out the car with my 38 in my hand. Cover me I said to Ready as I begin running up the hill in Beech Way apartments towards the gunshots. It had been cloudy all that day and it had just started to drizzle as I was running up the hill heading towards Caesars Ford apartments which was located right beside Beech Way. As I made it to the end of Caesars Ford apartments, I peeked my head around the apartment building at that moment I heard a loud boom which scared the s*** out of me and I jump back with my heart racing. What the f*** you scared of I heard Ready say as he ran up behind me it's only thunder n****I looked up at the sky and seen the clouds getting darker and darker. Within that split second we heard more gunshots. I looked around apartment building once again and seen two dark skin n***** shooting at my partner Kool-Aid.

40

The Hidden Valley Kings

Kool-Aid was ducked behind a white Cherokee and every second he'll pop up and let off a round or two. I ran out from side of the apartments with my 38 in hand and let off three shots as I ran towards the dumpster for cover. Ready stayed on the side of the apartment complex as he begins shooting at the dark skin n***** as well. I peeked around the dumpster and let off two more shots in the direction of one tall dark skin n****I heard Kool-Aid yell out that he was out of bullets I yelled back to him and told him that I was going to run towards him, and I asked Ready to cover me as I ran towards Kool-Aid. I let off one more shot and duck beside the Cherokee with my n****I can hear bullets penetrating the Cherokee that we were hiding behind I crawled on my belly towards the back end of the Cherokee and picked around the tire as I aim to pull the trigger, but nothing came out that's when I knew my chamber was empty damn, I said to Kool-Aid I'm out of bullets. I look back at Kool-Aid and realize he had been shot. I lean my back up against the back tire of the Cherokee as I dump the shells put them in my pocket and begin reloading my 38. As I put the last bullet into the chamber, I heard screeching tires that's when I looked up and seen a green Buick speeding out of Caesars Ford apartments I ran towards the Buick and squeezed off three shots Ready yelled to me that he was going to go and get the car and that he would be right back. I could hear sirens at a distance as I ran towards Kool-Aid to help my n**** up I threw Kool-Aid around my neck as I begin to half drag and half

41

carry him across the parking lot. Ready pulled up and helped me put Kool-Aid in the backseat. As we begin speeding out of Caesars Ford two or three police cars was coming towards us. Ready slowed down to not bring attention to us but the police cars turn right around and begin giving Chase. Ready smashed the gas speeding towards Sugar Creek Road. We made a short left on to Sugar Creek Road almost hitting another car. We continued down Sugar Creek running a red light crossing over North Tryon Street. By the time we got to the Plaza extension the rain was coming down pretty heavy. We crossed over the Plaza heading towards East way drive. Once we reached East way Ready made a sharp right turn which caused the car to spin around hitting another car. At that moment I was already jumping out the car running. I was finally captured on Grainger high school campus. I was handcuffed and dragged into the backseat of the police car. Yep, y'all boys really outdid yourself this time the police said as we were headed towards the station. Yep, you really f***** up. He continued and on about how we going to do life in prison. I zoned out looking up at the dark clouds as the rain continued to fall down. I was concerned about my partner Kool Aid knowing that he had been shot. I began thinking about everything that led up to my life at that point. All the fights all the shootouts and all the stress. Damn! is this the way I'm going to be for the rest of my life I remember thinking to myself. it wasn't long before we reached the police station. Sitting in the station the police tried everything possible to get information out of me which was hilarious and a waste of time. I finally fell asleep. I don't know how long I was out before being woken up by another officer. He grabbed a metal fold out chair and sat directly across from me. He scooted his chair up to the table and placed his hands on top of it. He stared at me for a moment and began to tap his fingers on the table. "Sir you are being charged with two counts of attempted murder, discharging a firearm in city limits, possession of a gun, reckless driving, and a list of other charges." I looked up at the ceiling, not saying a word. He became upset and slammed his palms on the table and pointed a finger at me." We have much evidence to put you away for a very long time. And if you don't start talking, I promise that I will personally see to it that you get everything that's coming to you." I continued to stare at the ceiling before answering. "I was just joy riding, don't know nothing about that other stuff" At the moment there was a knock on the door. The officer stood up to answer. A black man walked in and gave the officer a plastic bag. "Thanks sergeant" the officer said as the black man turned to leave. The officer walked back over to the table but didn't sit down. He had a smile on his face and began to pace back and forward. He stopped and looked at me again but this time his smile widened. He lifted up the plastic bag. "You see this? This here is called evidence and your fingerprints are all on it." I looked closely at the bag and noticed it held several shells of bullet casings. I shrug my shoulders and said," those not mine". He pointed

43

his finger again; look I'm not playing games with you. This is serious and I'm trying to help you. You do realize that two of those guys were shot up pretty badly and we believe that one isn't going to make. Now, we have your prints on the bag which is enough to put you away." He blew into his hands as if he was cold and continued. " If you help us, we will gladly let the judge know and your sentence will be much lighter. After all, we do have your prints so what's it going to be?" I was beginning to become irritated and was very tired. I started to get sleepy. I rubbed my eyes and looked at the officer. He stared at me with a smirk on his face. I guess he thought I was going to break. But I wasn't worried about his accusations. You see, I knew he didn't have my prints because I never load my weapons with bare hands. The only gun that they had was the gun that belonged to one of my homies who left it in the car a couple hours before the incident. No one's fingerprints were on the gun at least I knew mines wasn't. The other guns were tossed out and hasn't been recovered not to my knowledge. About two hours later another officer came into the room and began checking my hands for gun powder with some kind of tube I think it was a Q- tip. " This will tell it all" I remember the officer saying. I didn't know anything about gun residue around this time, so I asked the officer what he was doing. "This!" He said, "will determine if you fired a shot from any gun." This made me nervous because I knew I had been shooting. I tried to remain as calm as possible without showing signs of nervousness.

After the officer finished, he put the tube in a bag and then put the bag in a black box and left the room. " You see" said the officer who had been interrogating me. " We have much evidence and you better start cooperating, or you will live to regret it" The officer kept going on and on for about another hour until a black lady officer came into the room. "I need to speak with you sir" she said. The integrating officer slowly walked over to her. They began whispering amongst each other. "What! You got to be fucking kidding me" I heard the interrogating officer say." He looked back at me and stared. He turned back to the lady officer. "Where's the lieutenant!" he shouted. " I can't believe this shit". The lady officer left the room. A few minutes later a tall white man in a suit with a crew cut walked into the room. The interrogating officer began to say something, but the lieutenant stopped him. "We got to let him go, it's as simple as that" The interrogating officer shook his head." I can't believe this" he said. " Well believe it," said the lieutenant. " As a matter of fact, his mom is already here. The interrogating officer walked over to me. " I can't believe you only fourteen years old, but I'm going to come up with something. You are not walking out of here that easily ". He turned back to the lieutenant," sir this child still committed a crime we can't just let him walk". What are we going to charge him with?" Asked the lieutenant. "The guys who were dropped off at the hospital isn't talking, so we have nothing." The interrogating officer scratched his head and said, " what about the other charges that he's charged

45

with?" What about them asked the lieutenant? He's charged with a bunch of misdemeanors and a stolen car which doesn't qualify for incarceration at his age." This was music to my ears. I was released into the custody of my mother who almost immediately began beating my ass outside the police station while waiting on the bus. We finally made it home on the bus and I was tired from all the interrogation I had went through. It was almost midnight if my memory serves me correctly when we got home. I laid down to get some rest. I needed it. The next morning me and Ready went to look for the guns that the police didn't find. It took us hours to find those guns and we headed back to the hood. As soon as we reached the hood, we seen our crew standing at the top of Beech Way apartments and knew right away that something was wrong." What's up " asked Ready as we approach the homies." Man, these bitch ass n**** came through here busting at us!!" screamed Shine as he paced back and forth with a .45 in his hand. I looked at Roland as he and Kool Kat carried on a conversation. "It's on" I heard him tell Kool Kat. Everyone seemed hype except for me and Ready as we were still trying to figure out what the hell happened. Later on, we found out that some niggas tried to rob one of our people, but he took off running and the robbers began shooting at him. They tried to give chase but after the homies heard the shots, they came out the cut returning fire, causing the robbers to back up and retreat. In those days we stayed in beef with niggas who wanted our block because it was a gold mine. Kool-Aid recovered from his gunshot wounds and was back in action. We put the press on any and everybody. We were getting into shootouts left and right and we meant business.

Chapter 6

Nigga You Thought I Was Playing?

HIDDEN VALLEY ELEMENTARY SCHOOL I attended HIDDEN VALLEY ELEMENTARY SCHOOL in the third grade. I can't remember my teachers name, but she was a white lady. She also was very nice and concerned about us receiving the proper education. She had a very unique style in her teaching methods. She taught in a way that made us remember. It was in her class that I learned the names of all the states in America. She would write it as a song and have the class to sing it, so it was like remembering your favorite song. Throughout elementary school I stayed in fights. I remember this one fight I had with a guy who had just moved from Compton California, so he say. He was a lot bigger than me and older. I was in the fourth grade, and he was in the fifth. I forget what we fought about, and I was a little nervous because of his size. But once he threw that punch it was on. After that fight I felt invincible. Up until that point I really hadn't fought anyone good enough to say I was a great fighter. The fourth, fifth, and sixth would show my true fighting skills as I began fighting guys who had a name as being good fighters. Some I had a hard time with and even if they won, they would tell you they don't wish to fight me again. My fifth and sixth grade teachers had more of an impact on my life. They were the first black teachers I ever had, and they cared about all their students. They never gave up on me even when it appeared that I gave up on myself. I started selling drugs I'm the fifth grade. I was influenced by a friend from Harlem New York who was a successful hustler. This guy stayed fresh to death in Nike Flight Suits. And he wore Air Flight shoes with every outfit. Throughout my elementary school years, I dabble in selling drugs but wasn't successful. I believe I did it because it was cool. I never tried to save money. I remember in the sixth grade I started hustling on Amberly Lane and I had about 100 worth of rocks on me and this old head approach me saying I couldn't sell dope on that street because it was his block. I stayed because I needed to sell the shit I was given. About an hour later the old he pulled back up. " You still out here lil n****? I thought we had an understanding. If you still here when I get back, you are getting shot." He drove off burning rubber and I took off running back to Spring Gardens St. To the guys from New York. I told them what the old head said, and they told me to go back to the block and that I needed to learn how to stand my ground. They sent another guy back with me. The old head pulled back up aggressively and jumped out the car. "Nigga you thought I was playing" he said as he was gripping his gun. I looked at the older guy they sent back with me. He began talking to the guy with the gun, trying to calm him down. I don't remember what he said but I do know that the guy wasn't trying to hear it. So, I quickly out witted him." Man, we got Butcher Dollar shit" I remember saying. The guy looked at me for a moment and said "what did you just say" I repeated what I said. He looked at the ground and said, "I am going to holler at Butcher Dollar and see what's up". He jumped back in the car and speed off. I knew the old head and Butcher Dollar were partners in the drug trade, so I use that knowledge to my advantage. The old head never approach me again. Although I was dealing in drugs I still went to school. To me school was always fun. We used to have school dances in the cafeteria. It was a dollar to get in or you could bring can goods. There were many more activities such as book drives where we were allowed to receive new books that usually wasn't in the school library. Sometime around the sixth grade I began breaking into stores. B&E I remember the first time we broke into a store. Actually, it was Tryon Mall. Tryon Mall was a shopping center that had a few stores that sold urban fashions. I think they had a store called US FASHION another called HOLLOWAY. There was a record store and a couple littler stores. In fact, there was a club in the back. Attached to this shopping center was an Eckerd's drug store, Win Dixie, Family Dollar, and if my memory serves me correctly there was a PEOPLES store as well. Also, in this parking lot there was a bank, laundry mat and a movie theater called Tryon Mall. It was this very same movie theater we were headed to when we broke into our first store. I believe we was on our way to see New Jack City and we stopped at the shopping center to go window shopping. The mall was open, but all the stores were closed and the only person besides us was a janitor. We walked up to one of the stores and looked in. " Damn look at that Starter pull over jacket " one of my homies said. I walked over to the side of the window where he was standing and peered in. " Damn!! I agreed." It was an Oakland A's and I wanted it. Everyone had on a starter jacket except me. I kept staring at the jacket with lust. "I got to get this bitch" I said to no one in particular. As I was admiring the jacket, I noticed that the window had a small opening. It wasn't big enough for my arm to slip through, but I knew a stick would fit. I jogged to that back of the mall I stepped outside. There was a small, wooded area a few feet across the parking lot. I quickly went searching for a small but firm stick. After a few seconds I found what I was looking for and headed back into the mall. All five of my friends were waiting by the window. I walked up and slid the stick through the tiny slit. I was able to snatch the starter jacket off the rack but barely. I pulled and yank the jacket through the slit which was no easy task. I couldn't reach any of the others. But there were many nice things inside this store and there was no way to get inside. As we continue to press our faces up against the window, I heard someone say, " I'm going to find a brick ". The brick was thrown through the window and the alarm sounded so we all took off running. We ran out the mall into the parking lot. I threw on my nice new jacket, and we headed on to the movies. Some of the guys didn't have the money to get in and those of us who did sneaked the others in by opening the side emergency door. After watching New Jack City, we went into the game room.

They had plenty of games to choose from, but my favorite was King of the Ring. For some

reason I could never beat the guy that looked like Mike Tyson. We finally got tired of playing video games and decided to leave. It was late in the evening when we all walked outside. Once we got outside, we could still hear the alarm ringing loud and clear. But we also noticed that there were no cop cars around. We walked back to the mall and looked inside. The alarm was still ringing loudly. One of the guys said" let's see if we can get in." We began to find different ways to get in. The entrance to the mall was locked. But we knew that the store window we busted had to be unprotected because the alarm was still ringing, and no police had shown up. As everyone continued to try and come up with a way to get inside, one of the homies asked if someone would help lift him up to see if he can go through the roof after several unsuccessful attempts, we gave that idea up. We continued to brainstorm. Someone began to rub their hands across the wide entry window. Man, this ain't even plexiglass. It's real glass. At that moment everyone was excited because we knew a glass window only needed a hefty brick. One of went around back to look for one. But I said fuck it and ran a shopping cart through the window.

Seconds later we were storming the mall like swat. We ran to the store that had the busted window. In matter of seconds, we were all inside grabbing any and everything. I grabbed so much shit that I had to use a shopping cart. Others began to put their shit in shopping carts as well. We all left running out of Tryon Mall parking lot pushing our carts across North Tryon Street on to Welling Ford Street in Hidden Valley. As we were going down the street there was a robbery going on in one of the trap houses. Some Jamaicans was robbing two older cats because this trap house was doing numbers. As I ran past the house a shootout started and I can hear the bullets zooming past my ears. It was so much commotion. There were Jamaicans who were trying to snatch our shit while they homies were shooting into the house. Shit was crazy. It seemed like more and more Jamaicans were jumping out the van shooting. I kept pushing my cart with my head down running full speed. With us running with shopping carts full of stolen clothes and all the shooting it looked like a riot. People were shooting into the house and my man cousin was shooting out the house. Through all the chaos I finally made it home with my goods. The next day I learned about what happened involving the shootout. A guy from Grier Town had come and posted up for a couple of days and was grinding with my older homies at the house. After he seen how much money was being made, he one day tied up a friend of mines who was there by himself and made all the money. Later that day when the guys pulled up the nigga snuck out the back door leaving the homie tied up. And that's where the homies found him. Tied up and gagged but unharmed. We were sitting on the porch as my older homie told us the story. "Man, after we found this nigga tied up, we knew it was going to be a war. Either we were going take it to them or they were coming back. The nigga came back with so many Jamaicans." The homie took a pull from his cigarette and continued. "Man, I was in the kitchen cooking up when my man come running in the house calling my name and as soon as he was in the door, I heard the shots. I ducked low and grabbed the .357 off the stove and crawled to the window. I began busting back but I was outnumbered. Then I heard a loud boom. I thought they was coming through the back door, but I later found out that the homie had dived in the tub." We all started laughing. He continued with the story and we all just listened.

ROBBED AT GUNPOINT 1991 and me It was Halloween night, and me and the guys were on our way to the Hidden Valley Elementary school dance with our can goods to get in with. I was wearing my Oakland A's Starter jacket that I've taken from the mall along with my all white Buffalo shoes which was also taken from mall. We all left my house and headed towards the path at the church that leads us to the next street called Kentbrook which was behind the school. As we were approaching the path a car pulled up on church grounds and four niggas hopped out with guns. They robbed us of our stolen merchandise and hopped back in the car and pulled off. We never made it to the dance since we were all robbed at gun point. I was pissed off and wanted revenge in the worst way. That revenge came about a month later. Me and the guys were standing on the corner of Wellingford and Hersey Street when a guy was walking from the corner store with a lady and child. I didn't recognize him but one of the homies did. "Man, that's one of them niggas that robbed us" he said. At first, I wasn't sure, but my man surety convinced me. None of us had a gun as we watched him, and his family walk past us going up Hersey Street. "Man, I wish I had a gun" said one of the guys. We looked on helplessly as the guy walked further up the street. "Fuck it lets beat his ass" I said but everyone was against it saying he might be packing a pistol, especially if he's a stick-up kid. As we continued to watch him get further away, an older guy from North Charlotte that we sold dope for pulled up in a black Feira.

The homie ran up to his car and asked the older homie for a pistol. He was reluctant at first, but the homie kept pressing saying the guy robbed us and that he took the money that was owed to the older hustler. This was a lie since the homies had fucked up the pack before the robbery.

The older guy said, " I'll give the gun to Roscoe because he seems to have the heart to actually carry it out". I was given a small 25 automatic and we all jogged to catch up with the robber.

Once we got up on him, I pulled out the pistol." What you didn't think we would recognize your bitch ass" the lady began screaming and pleading for his life. She claimed that he was with her the entire day of Halloween. She was so convincing that I began to have doubts. But I didn't want to look like a punk, so I put all reason to the side and started shooting at his foot after I ran out of bullets, I started running in the opposite direction towards Wellingford St. " Man you ain't hit

shit" one of the guys said. "None of you n**** had the balls to do nothing" the older hustler said as I returned the gun back to him. The guys kept saying what they would have done if they were given the gun. They went on and on. About two hours later a car pulled up and an older dude hopped out with a gun and told me not to move. I froze. It was the guy I shot at girlfriend brother. My heart dropped and I didn't have a weapon. " Damn!" I said to myself. The other guys took off running at left me. I stood there trapped. I had to think quick because this nigga was screaming and acting crazy. I kept trying to plead with him at least long enough until I figured something out. Several cars were turning off of Spring View rd. on to Welling Ford Street. Me and the guy was standing on Springview but the part that was further up in Beech Way. I noticed about three cars kept straight on Springview crossing over Wellingford into Beech Way. The cars had to slow down because we were standing in the middle of the street and his car was also parked in the street. I was facing the traffic while he faced me, so his back was to the traffic. He couldn't see the cars, but he heard them. That's when I said " everything is ok officer" the guy eyes grew big as he began slowly putting the gun into his belt. He slowly turned his head and body in the direction that he thought the cop car was. That's when I struck out running full speed heading towards the creek. As soon as I hit the creek, I heard the gunshots. I kept running across the creek and jumped a fence into a friend back yard which led me to another street called Cinderella. As I was walking, I remembered thinking about my niggas Ready and Roland. I knew for sure they wouldn't have left me for dead like them other niggas. Ready and Roland had moved to Pits Drive off of Beatties Ford Road. Damn I miss my brothers. I didn't know where the others went so, I headed on home. Another B&E We continued to break in the same store repeatedly until we were finally captured. We may break into that store a dozen times before the police actually apprehended us. Well, we were caught once before, but it was at the store.

This happened all the way across town. We had just broken in one of the stores and loaded the merchandise into a stolen van. We then proceeded to Wilkerson Blvd in hopes to break into Hyatt's Gun Shop. We pulled into the parking lot and drove straight up to the front entrance.

Everyone hopped out and ran up to peek inside. We began plotting on how to get inside. "This shit go be hard" I said, and everyone agreed. " Man, I got to take a shit." One of the homies said. " Well how you go do that ain't no bathroom out here nigga." I said as the homie looked at me with a frown. " Fuck this shit, it got to be some napkins in the van, I got to shit bad". He headed to the van and I yelled out to him " use some leaves mother fucker" and everyone started laughing. We continued to brainstorm as the homie went around the back of the store. As we were all standing around, the police pulled into the parking lot." Damn!" I said as the cop car got closer. Instead of us all just walking away from the store and stolen van, we decided to jump back in the van and pulled off. The police followed us out the parking lot. We turned onto Wilkerson Blvd and headed towards the airport. The police were still behind us. "Switch lanes" I said. I wanted to see if we were being followed. Sure, enough the police switch lanes as well. "Switch again" someone said. And the driver did so. The police switch again. It was no doubt they were on to us plus the van was stolen. The driver mashed the gas, and the chase was on. We continued to drive up Wilkerson at a high speed until we somehow turned down a street that wasn't actually a street but a dead end. We were trapped with nowhere to go. It was about 2 am and the street lit up with cop cars blocking us in. We had lots of stolen merchandise inside a stolen van. "Put your hands where we can see them" I heard a cop say. I tried to hide under all the stolen clothes that was in the van as they began snatching everyone out one by one. I was the last one in the van since I was hiding. I remain under all the clothes in hopes of being overlooked. I could hear the officer re-entering the van I could feel his presence. I could also see the light from his flashlight although it appeared dim because I was still under the clothes. I felt the officers weight shift as he stood beside me. My heart started racing and was beating so hard I could hear it thumping in my ears. The fear of being caught made me want to jump up and try to make a run for it but that same fear kept me frozen under the clothes. I felt the shift and I knew another officer had entered the van. " I don't see no one else" I heard an officer say. But at that moment, almost the same time he spoke, he stepped on my leg. " What the hell is that" I heard a voice.

The clothes were snatched back, and my face was flooded with bright lights. "Don't move son of bitch" I heard the officer say. I tried to shield the lights from my eyes as the officers began grabbing me." We have another one". They snatched me up after putting on the cuffs and dragged me out the van. I see the other homies all lined up sitting on the ground side by side in a row. They put me with the others. There we were all lined up with about 10 officers standing

over us and asking questions. They started separating us so each officer could speak with us individually. After about a good 20 minutes they bring us all back together. " So, we know that there is one more of you that wasn't in the van." One of the officers said. I'm thinking to myself " how the fuck they know that" I looked to my left and seen the lil homie dozing off. He had been drinking MAD DOG (MD 2020) and I could tell it was hitting him hard at this moment. I wondered how long the cops was going to keep us out here. About 5 minutes later another patrol car pulled up with the homie. He wasn't in the van because he went around back to take a shit while the rest of us was trying to figure out how to get inside the store and when the cops pulled up, we all jumped in the van and forgot the homie. The cops had the homie in the backseat and let him out but kept him standing by the back door or the patrol car on the driver side. "Do any of you know him" the policeman asked us. We all said no. "Are y'all sure" he asked again. Everyone agreed that we never seen him before. Just when they were about to let him go the drunken lil homie beside me began to stir and he lifted his head and squinted his eyes in the other homie direction. " The caught you too J ?" The lil homie asked. Not knowing that he just got the homie a charge. Calling out his name confirmed that he was who the police was looking for. I could see the anger in J eyes as he looked at the lil homie in disbelief. After that, the cops started putting us into separate police cars and we all headed downtown. They put us all in separate rooms and started the interrogation process. After a few hours most of us were released because we were juveniles. Two of the homies were left behind because they were sixteen and seventeen respectfully. After being released I took the number 11 city bus home.

We had broken into the mall so many times that by the time we were captured, I believe I was charged with over seven B&E, s. We always picked the weekend. But this one weekend didn't feel right. I remember everyone being excited about breaking into the mall again. But my nerves were a wreck. I couldn't put my finger on it, but I was uncomfortable. It was a Saturday night and we headed back to the mall. We decided to go around back. We had gone around back the last few times because it was out of people sight. When we approach the rear, we noticed that the window we previously broke was boarded up. We all began to pull on the board. After about a good three minutes I thought I seen I shadow inside the mall. "I must be seeing things" I said to myself. I continued to help pull the board down and seen the shadow again. " Man, somebody in there!" I yelled to the others. Everyone stopped what they were doing and looked. There was no shadow this time. "This nigga scared" one of the homies said.

Everyone started laughing and continued to pull on the board. "Man, I saw something" I said feeling embarrassed and angry. " Man, you go help us get this shit off or what" the homie asked. I began helping to pull on the board. Again, I saw something and stopped. I stared at the spot where I thought I seen something. Everyone noticed that I've stopped. But they continued pulling and cracking jokes at me. The shadow reappeared but this time I seen it. It was a white man peeking around the corner of one of the stores and he was speaking into a walkie talkie." Oh shit, it's the police in there" I whispered to the others. "Roscoe tripping and seeing shit" someone said. "I'm getting out of here" I said. I started heading towards the small, wooded area behind the mall. I noticed J was following me. As soon as we reached the woods, I could hear screeching tires and the back of the mall was flooded with police lights. Somehow J and I separated momentarily. I was taking baby steps in hopes to not give myself away by stepping on a branch. As I walked further, I seen what looked like a cop. I froze, afraid to move. I could see what looked like a police hat and a badge on his jacket. He began to walk towards me and just when I was about to run, I heard him whisper my name. I looked harder and realized it was J. His outfit looked like a police uniform in the dark. He had on a Raiders cap and a Raiders jacket. The silver Raiders logo looked like badges in the dark. " J is that you" I whispered. "Yea it's me, we got to get out of here. Where the fuck those police come from?" "Man, I told them niggas I seen someone in the mall. They wouldn't listen". I spoke. J turned and started heading towards the other end of the woods. I followed. After about two minutes we came out behind Auto zone and walked towards North Tryon Street. It wasn't long before we had a good distance between us and the police. Since I was close to home, I told J I would see him later. For some reason after doing dirt, I always felt that home was a safe haven. Even when I ran from the police, I would go home knowing the cops knew where I lived. But it was home that made me feel safe. I later learned that me and J were the only ones to get away. Another homie had gotten away but was arrested after he went downtown with his mom to pick up his brother who was caught. In order for the cops to know he was there meaning someone gave up all our names.

Chapter 7

My Probation

This was confirmed when I was arrested at Street Academy, a school for troubled kids. I was released in my mom's care but this time I had to go to juvenile court and was given one year probation. After I was given probation, I was in and out of Gatlin Detention Center for violating my probation. Gatlin is a detention center for young juveniles, and they had girls also. The first time I violated I was made to do a weekend. After that my time was never less than two weeks. Every time I went to Gatlin it seemed like someone was always testing my boxing skills. Gatlin consisted of robbers, murderers, rapists etc. There was a mixture of just bad as kids. Who were still immature and gave each other the blues? I remember one day getting into fight with two guys from West Blvd. One was a light skin kid named T with funny colored eyes. The other whose name I don't recall was a tall dark skin kid. I really don't remember how the fight started but I do know that there was three of them at first. Can't remember the description of the other kid. We were in the laundry closet getting our boxers, socks, etc. when an argument began. I don't know what the argument was about, but I do remember throwing the first punch. I was then jumped. The third guy who description I can't recall, had run off. The fight only lasted about 40 seconds in which the staff came running to break it up. There was one kid who did jump in to help. I believe he was from North Charlotte. Also, there was a very close friend of mine from Hidden Valley who was in on a murder charge, but he didn't budge to help. Instead, he gave praise only fighting. They put us in lock up which was our cell. I think we stayed locked down for a day. I was then released about a week later. Again, I was back on the streets getting into more bullshit. It wasn't long before we broke into another establishment. MY FIRST SO-CALLED BID I continued to do dumb shit until I violated my probation. I was then sent to Mills Group Home located in Thomasville North Carolina. Mills was a place for troubled kids, and many other things. It was set up like a small community. There were a few streets with nice homes. These homes were where the kids lived. We had a gym, swimming pool and was given a weekly allowance in which we went skating every weekend. We also were allowed to go to the mall. We took trips to the beach etc. It was like summer camp to me. We had chores around the house, and we were allowed to visit other homes. It was here when I first started smoking. I still remember when a native American handed me a cigarette. It was late in the evening, and we had just finished eating. The native American pulled out some cigarettes and asked if I smoke, I told him no and he offered me one. Try it out it will relieve some stress. I grabbed a cigarette. I believe it was a Camel cigarette. After that first pull, I was dizzy as hell. But I must admit, it felt good. The home I was in had about seven or eight children that lived there. It was all boys. They kept the boys and girls separated. The girls had their own homes as did the boys. However, we were allowed to kick it with the girls. For some reason the staff looked at me as the troublemaker. This was far from the truth. Like much of my life, I was provoked. The difference between me and a lot of guys is that I always finish what they started. And then they go report me to the police, CO,s Staff etc. I remember this one time an older guy tried to crack jokes and I told him that I was far from a clown so find someone else to joke with. After about 45 seconds of him still taunting me, I decided to swing. We were standing at the top of the stairs when I punched him.

This was bad. The guy went tumbling down the stairs. After landing at the bottom, he remained still. "Shit he's dead" I heard someone say. I walked down the steps and stood over him. He wasn't moving". Damn how in the hell I got this much bad luck" I remember saying to myself. I ran back upstairs and started packing my clothes. "I'm getting the fuck out of here". After grabbing my clothes out the dresser I asked one of my partners to go sneak me some trash bags. As I waited on the bags, I heard voices downstairs. I stood up and was about to approach the top of the steps when I heard footsteps coming up. I looked towards the window and decided to jump out. As I ran back to the room I went for the window. As I was lifting it up, I heard Mrs. K voice. " Roscoe why did you do this" I looked over my shoulder and was relieved to see the kid I punch standing next to her. He was bruised a little, but alive. After the incident I was told that I was no longer welcomed they're and that my case worker was on his way to take me to training school. About 3 hours later my case worker showed up. His name was Tony, and he was Italian. He was cool as fuck and was always in my corner. He had a street like mentality. Once he arrived, I was called downstairs with my clothes in bags ready to go to training school. However, Mr. T had some questions for the staff who acted as our guardians. The conversation lasted probably 20 minutes. All I remember Mr. T saying is "so you all are telling me that the only witness is the victim himself and no one else seen anything?" Mrs. K said that there was a witness and called for the guy who screamed out that the guy was dead. Mr. T question him as well. He asked the kid if he seen me push or throw the boy down the stairs. He admitted that he only seen the kid laying at the bottom of the steps and that I had ran downstairs to look at him. So, Mr. T called me over and asked if I assaulted the kid and I denied it. Mr. T then looked at Mrs. K and shrugged his shoulders. "There's no witnesses and I can't take him to Training School based off one kid who's the victim word" he said. I was able to stay at Mills Group

Home to finish out my sentence of three months. Everything went pretty smooth after that, and I even got a girl. She was white and very quiet. She was nice but we had to keep it a secret because she said her father didn't like black people. Everything was pretty good up until the day they took all us kids to the public library. We were all told to find a book to read. Everyone went their separate ways in search. I looked at a few books but none of them I liked. As I was about to give up, I seen one particular book that stood out. It was a black book with a large red "X" on it. I grabbed the book and looked at the back cover. As I read the back cover, I noticed that Malcom was once a criminal. This intrigued me to read the book even more. I took the book to Mrs. K so she could check it out. When she seen the book and the tittle, I noticed she looked uncomfortable. She slowly reached for the book and began thumbing through it. She then looked at me and said she know of a better book. She claimed I would be just as excited about this book as well. She turned and stormed off. After about two minutes she came back with a book. "Here you go, give this a try". I reached for the book, and it was on Martin Luther king Jr. I flipped through the pages and wasn't interested. " I don't want this one, give me the one with the X on it. She looked a little upset, but she handed me back Malcolm. "You sure you don't want the book about Martin Luther king?" Mrs. K asked." He's more appropriate and plus a loving Christian". "Nah, I want this one" I said. I checked out Malcom X and happily walked back to the van to wait on the others. As I sat in the van, I started reading my book. I was on the second or third page when everyone started getting into the van. Mrs. K paused and looked at me and then she looked at the book I was holding. I noticed her face was red. " What's up with her and this book" I said to myself. It was the way she acted that made me want to get the book even more. I never finished reading Malcolm. At that time, I wasn't really into reading. I grabbed Malcom because I see how upset it made the staff. Plus, I don't even remember learning about Malcolm in school. It was always Martin. However, over the years I will become very familiar with Malcom. I believe I was released sometime in August 1992.

Chapter 8

Tom Hunter Rd

REUNITED After my release I found out that my best friend Ready and his brother Rolland had moved back to the Valley. This time they moved on Pondella Rd. I must admit that I was very excited about reuniting with my homie. I forgot how I found out what street he lives on, but someone told me, and I remember going to their house early the next morning. We talked about the things we've been through since we've been separated, and they told me that they were living on Pitts Drive and had gotten into the dope game. Ready was doing okay for himself he was buying a quarter ounce which was 7 grams and back then the price for that was $350. But I've seen people cut up $900 worth, so you were damn near tripling your money. I told them how I had to do 2 months at a group home and how the other friends I started hanging out with wasn't built like them and that I missed them and was glad to be reunited once again. They told me about new n****** that they had met while living off Beatties Ford Road. They told me these guys were soldiers. I started going to Ready and Rolland house pretty much

70

every day. Our bond grew stronger and stronger as we fought alongside of each other against our adversaries. At this time the only people that were a part of our crew was me, ready Rolland, their cousin Prophecy and they're half-brother Homes, Fruit and Kool-Aid. We were beginning to be a force to reckon with. We didn't have many guns only a couple and we used to take turns on who would carry them. I remember one day me Rolland and his older brother Homes had walked from Ready and Rolland house to go visit our homeboy Fruit on White plains. As we walked up Pondella Rd. We began discussing how to get more guns because we had just gained a new enemy and they wasn't bull shitting. As we turned on Bilmark heading toward Echo Glen we continued our conversation. It wasn't long before we finally reached Tom Hunter. As we turned on Tom Hunter Road, I seen something laying in the street, so I approached the object and seen that it was a pair of brand-new pants with the price tag still on them I thought maybe someone has stolen them and drop them as they were running. I went and picked up the pants and noticed that the pants felt kind of heavy I told my homies it's something in the pants pocket I reached in the pocket and pulled out a 38 revolver it was black. I quickly put the 38 on my waist and threw the pants over my shoulders. Roland looked at me and said "damn n**** you going to keep the pants" "hell yeah" I said. Roland shook his head, and we continue heading towards fruit house. Homes kept trying to convince me to give him the 38 and he would give me a saw off 12 gauge when we got back to the crib. I quickly disagreed saying I can keep the 38 concealed how the f*** I'm going to keep a 12-gauge concealed n**** you crazy. We argued all the way to fruit house. Homes kept trying to all the good things the 12 gauge could do for me, but I wasn't listening. We finally made it to Fruit house. When we arrive, Fruit was bumping EPMD. We all sat down and rolled up a Philly blunt. We chopped it up for about an hour or two before we left. Fruit couldn't leave because he had to watch his younger brother C. Me Roland and his brother Homes started walking back up Tom Hunter. We were all high and in our own thoughts we were so spaced out in our own thoughts that we were no longer walking together. Homes was in the front Rowland was about 10 to 12 ft behind him and I was a few feet behind Roland. Roland wanted to stop in Somerset apartments to holler at a friend of his. As we walk into Somerset apartments a green lowrider pickup truck pulled up on me and an older dude hopped out back of the truck bed and approach me. But he approached me in an aggressive manner asking me what the f*** I was doing with his pants as he was questioning me about three or four more guys hopped off the back of the truck, I quickly reached on my hip pulled out the 38. I quickly aim and pull the trigger, but nothing came out. The guys rush me and grab me slinging me up against the fence. They begin wrestling with me trying to take the gun out my hand. Roland and his brother Homes were ahead of me zoned out and didn't know what

was transpiring. I screamed out Roland name and
he turned around quickly and when he seen what
was happening, he started running towards us.
Roland begins throwing people off of me with the
help from his brother. Somewhere along the
struggle I dropped the gun and a skinny n*****
picked it up. The skinny n***** then ran over to
where Roland was at to help one of his homeboys
that Roland was punishing. Two more guys wrestle
me to the ground, and I was pent and couldn't
move. I looked up to see Roland given two n*****
the business I couldn't see where Homes was
because the guys had me pent on my stomach
and I couldn't see behind me I continue to
struggle trying to get up but couldn't. After about
2 to 3 minutes the skinny n***** who picked up
the gun became infuriated that they couldn't take
Roland down. He ran to the truck reached inside I
really couldn't see what he was grabbing because
I couldn't turn my head, I had to cut my eyes, but
it appeared that he grabbed some bullets because
he started loading the empty 38 with intention on
shooting Roland. However, an older guy finally got
out the truck and told the skinny n*****" nah lil
bro that man got heart fight him straight up".
However, the skinny n***** wasn't trying to hear
that and him and the older guy began arguing. As
the guys let me up off the ground, they all began
walking towards the older guy and threw all this
madness a few more guys came out of Silverstone
apartments and they all had guns in their hands,
but nobody made a move it appeared the older
guy was the leader, and they did what he said do

but the skinny n***** seem to challenge his authority. Later on, we will soon find out that the skinny n***** name was Snake, and the older guy was his big brother named Big Snake and they hung out at Cedar Green Apartments. After Big Snake calmed everyone down, they started piling back in the low rider truck and the guys that had come out the apartments vanished. Once they left, we ran to Roland's friend apartment in Summer Set. Once inside we immediately started plotting. We caught a ride to Briscoe house on Thorn Wood in the hood. This is where we kept our guns. We called up Kool-Aid, Ready and fruit. All three came to the house and we made further plans on how to get back at Snake and their crew. a few weeks would go by before Roland and a couple homies will run into snake and his crew at Eastland Mall. A little scuffle broke out but nothing too serious. We were all young between the ages of 13 and 18 and was doing what most young black teenagers do in which we considered as fun. But make no mistake about it some of us kids could be deadly. This was in the 90s. The '90s was a war zone for black men and children in the city of Charlotte. It appeared everyone was dying throughout the city. And the crack error was hitting hard in the '90s.It was a lot more violence back then because everyone was hustling out in the open which made it easy for the ops to run up on you and the stick-up kids to jump out on you. But one thing that stood out that none of this new era has experience (due to their poor character and lack of respect for the game) is that everyone was making money n****** was making so much money back then that even the hustle God had to smile. Also, a lot more people was jumping off the porch at a much younger age. I'm talking about starting at the age of 10. Back then it wasn't unusual to see a kid in elementary with about 200.00$ in his pocket. It was so much dope in the city back then that I remember times on a few occasions that I've been walking down the street and come across about three or four squares

dime bags of crack scattered out on the ground. This was normal back then. You would see paraphernalia all out in the street. Whether it was on the block in front of the corner store or even in someone's yard. The '90s era was also the era with famous notorious Jack boys. In my opinion the hustlers of today wouldn't have stood a chance in the '90s era. There was almost just as many jack boys then there were hustlers. You had Jack-boys like Avalot, Maverick, Keenan, David Crockett, Mike-Mike, so many others whose names would be a book in itself dead or alive. And if you weren't about that gun play stay your ass on the porch. Even n****** that was considered Soft in the game was forced to bust they guns every now and then. Gun Play After the Eastland Mall incident it was time to get more guns. The only problem was we didn't have the finances to get such artillery. One day we were all chilling at Briscoe house and put all the guns on the bed that we owned. As we all stood around looking down at the weapons, we knew just how important it was to get more weapons. Among the six of us we only had three guns. A raggedy 38 that Kool-Aid had. The 38 was so busted up that he had to use a piece of clothes hanger to keep the barrel from falling out. But that 38 got us out of a lot of jams. Also, we had a 45 caliber and a 12-gauge sawed off. The way s*** was going we was in desperate need of guns. We had planned to break in this pawn shop in hopes to retrieve guns and ammunition. But somehow on our way we got pulled over by the cops and everyone jumped out and ran. Me and Ready were caught were actually Ready was caught and when I went back to double check on him and tried to figure out a way to get him out the back seat I was spotted and also tackled. If my memory served correctly, I don't think they locked us up I believe they let us go after all we was never caught inside the car. A few days have gone by before Ready and them moved off Pondella and back into Caesars Ford apartments. It was around this time that I met High Times through Ready and Rolland. He was a light skin cat with broad shoulders and a low haircut. I remember getting into a fight with High Times not long after I have met him. We got into an argument inside of Ready and Rolland apartment and I rushed them pushing him up against the refrigerator. Roland got in between us and told us to take it outside. Once outside we locked in like Pitbull's. After that day me and High Times were pretty cool. I had a habit of testing new members in our circle whether they were bigger than me or older than me I tried them. So now the circle was Me, Ready, Roland, Homes, High Times, Fruit and Briscoe. This was the early

90s and we were at war with different groups. We all used to post up in Beachway and Cesar Ford apartments kicking the b*******. Some of us sold dope because others posted up with pistols. Since we were little there were a portion of us that was hustlers and another portion that was gangsters, but we all got down when necessary. One day we were all chilling at Briscoe house when Roland and Fruit came rushing into the house. They both went straight to the mattress, and each grab a weapon. I asked Roland what was going on and Fruit answered, "them n***** y'all ran into in Silver Stones is up at Tom Hunter Park right now." The homies loaded up in a stolen Jeep and headed towards Tom Hunter Park. I had to sit this one out because the homies said they wanted to see what Fruit was made of he hadn't put in any work as of yet. So, the homies drove away four deeps because the rest of us stayed behind. About an hour later the homies pulled up in a different car. They begin telling us how everything went down and how they represented for the hood. After that it seems as if we stay in shootouts. One day we were all walking looking for a car to steal when Ready decided that we should go to the car lot on North Tryon beside Canterbury Woods. We had walked from Beachway all the way to Canterbury woods. As we walk through Canterbury woods there were two guys sitting on the steps in front of their apartment. I don't remember what caused the argument, but words were exchanged, and I believe one of my homies pulled out a weapon. The two guys quickly ran upstairs inside their apartment. We didn't think anything of it and continued on our mission in search for a car. The car lot had security patrolling it and we could see them yards away. So, we decided to head back down towards Beach way. Instead of walking the same route we came decided to circle around the other way. And it was a good thing that we did because we saw the two guys that we were arguing with running in the direction that they see us going but they had guns out. They were trying to sneak up behind us and I guess they're intention was to start shooting from the back but by us circling around we end up damn near behind them. My homie Ike, who was with us, was the first to notice. Mike pointed and said" look! them n***** trying to creep up". Everyone looks in the direction he pointed to and seen the n****** jogging in the way they seen us go. This time they had a third guy with them. Roland was the first one to react and started jogging lightly as if on his tippy toes behind the three guys. Everyone else did the same thing. However, Kool-Aid was the first to start shooting. I see the three guys scatter and take cover. We had a real live shootout right there in Canterbury Woods apartments. Me and my partner Hightower took cover on someone's back porch. The back porch had something like a wooded in fence with chicken screen. The bullets were penetrating the wood, so it wasn't much shelter, but it was better than no shelter at all. At least they couldn't see exactly where we were located because of the solid what it fences but they knew we was behind it, so they kept shooting in our direction. The other homies took cover behind trees. Every few seconds I will stick my arm out over the wooded fence and let off his shot without looking while still being crouched. The shootout didn't last that long probably 45 seconds at the most. My homie Hightower wasn't strapped and laid on his stomach while the shooting was going on. After I ran out of bullets, I too lay down beside him on my stomach waiting for the shooting to stop which seems as if it had no ending. The bullets kept piercing the wood as the debris from the wood flew on top of our heads and body. As We lay on our stomachs, I heard my homie Ike scream out to Kool-Aid to make a run for it. I couldn't see but I knew Kool-Aid did just that then I heard him call out all of our names to do the same.

Me and Hightower booted from the porch and as we ran, I could see Ike holding the guys at Bay with a 45 caliber. Me and the rest of the homies ran out on to Tom Hunter Road in the middle of the street a few seconds later Ike come running from around the apartments putting his gun inside his leather trench jacket. No one was injured on either side. We all headed back towards the block in Beachway apartments. We still wanted a car, so Kool-Aid and Ike went by themselves and came back an hour later with a 1990 Buick. Four of us jump inside the car and went on our missions. Me, Kool-Aid and ready always use the cars to put in work. Roland Ike Hightower and High time always use the car to go get p**** because they were older than us and was always chasing girls while the younger crew was chasing down ops. After we jumped in the car, we had it towards West boulevard on the west side of Charlotte. Kool-Aid had beef on that side of town, and he wanted to cruise that area in hopes of running into his ops, so we all headed in that direction strapped and loaded. After riding around for an hour, we decided to head back to the hood. A few days have gone by after the shootout in Canterbury Woods apartments and some of the homies were still a little pissed off about it and decided to return to finish the job. As they were discussing the situation me and Ready decided to Joy Ride and left the older guys behind to figure out what they're going to do. We roll All over the north side of Charlotte doing donuts and burnouts having fun in someone else's car not caring if we wrecked or not. After having reckless fun, we decided to go grab a beer neither one of us had money, so I had to walk into the BP store grab a case of beer and ran out to the car without paying I hop in the car, and we burnt out. Ready wasn't a drinker and by the time we got to the hood I had down four cans of beer and was drunk as hell. Once we made it to the hood, I told Ready to go back through Canterbury Woods to see if we see them n****** standing outside again. We cruised up Tom Hunter. Headed towards Canterbury Woods I rolled my window down preparing myself to shoot out the passenger window as we got closer to the apartment complex, we seen people standing outside. Once we turned on Canterwood Drive, we seen polices and ambulance. People were all standing around trying to see what happened I told Ready to keep going and not to stop. Ready looked at me and said, "nigga I already know that s***". "S*** n**** I can't tell your ass was slowing down" I said. We Begin arguing all the way back to the block. Once we pull back into the apartments, we seen the older homies standing outside chopping it up. "What up with y'all", I asked as me and Ready was leaving the car. Roland and Kool-Aid were arguing when we approached." What's I'm going on" Ready asked. Ike looked at Ready shaking his head. "Man, your brother and Kool-Aid went back to Canterbury Woods and shot up the complex and Roland told Kool-Aid to drive but Kool-Aid wanted to shoot so he was driving while trying to shoot and wrecked the car and they had to jump out and run-on feet back to the block. "After about 3 to 5 minutes of arguing Kool-Aid stormed off. I asked him where he was going, and he said to get another car. The next day we were all chilling on the block when an Escort GT turned into the apartments. We all kept our eye on the car as it went to the top of Beech Way and made a U- turn. Our complex was a dead end. As everyone was watching the car, I noticed that my girlfriend little brother had got on his bike and was riding around in circles in the parking lot at the top of Beachway. "What's up lil Paco, where is your sister, "I asked why keeping my eyes on the car. The car started creeping back down going back the way it came in. Some of us were standing at the bottom of Beachway and others was at the top. As the car continue to cruise by shots rained out. Everyone didn't have guns but those of us who did return fire. It only lasted about 15 seconds. When the shooting stopped, someone asked where Paco was. At that moment Kool-Aid came strolling down the hill. "Everybody cool" he asked. We all nodded. "Man, I couldn't get off like I wanted to because I had to move Paco out way" Kool-Aid continued. "So, Paco straight" Roland asked. "Yeah, he straight". "Man, who the fuck was that?" Ready asked as we all begin to leave the scene. Everyone headed towards Briscoe house on Thorn Wood. We Begin planning retaliation as soon as we made it to Briscoe's. Locked back up. I was still on probation and was still constantly fucking up. I had a court date and didn't bother to show up. A warrant was issued for my arrest. Every day the cops drove through the block looking for me.

This made the block hot. The cops knew they would see me if they just drove pass at least twice a day. I continued to hang on the block knowing I had warrants. This was around the time Shug and his brother Nyland started coming around. I been knowing Shug from Hidden Valley Elementary school. But we weren't that close at that time. I had met Shug and Black Travis through my friend Keenan Davis who I was pretty close to. But we were all in elementary school then. Now we were young teenagers. A couple of weeks after Shug and his brother started coming around, Shug went to prison for a while. Nyland came around a few times but not as much as Shug. I remember Shug being one of the first people to front me dope. I was in the sixth grade. I used to page him from the principal office every day. He gave me work up until the point I jumped the fence on him. After being on the run a couple of months our circle got a little bigger. It was now me, Ready, Roland, Hightower, High Times, Ike, Briscoe, Kool-Aid, Shug, Nyland, and Boskee and his crew. This was around the time we became Vice Lord's. It was around the beginning of 93 and we were all chilling on the block when we noticed a group of niggas hanging in front of Beech Way apartments on the bottom. "Man, who the fuck is them niggas" Roland asked pulling on a Newport. Everyone turned their attention towards the group of niggas. "I don't know but they better not be hustling out here" I heard Ready say. We all continued to study the group. They were extremely loud and animated. A few were drinking beer and causing a scene. We all kept our eyes on them and every now and then they would lock eyes with us. "Who the fuck them niggas looking at?" I asked gripping the 38. "Just chill" Kool- Aid said to me. " Man, fuck chill. They act like they have a problem" I started to walk towards them but Ready grabbed my arm. "We got to see what they on first". After about 10 or 15 minutes seen a junkie walk up and one of the guys served him. "Man, you see that s***" asked High Times. "Everybody loads up", said Roland. I pulled out my 38 "s*** I'm already strapped "as I begin walking towards the guys with my gun in hand. "Yo 'Scoe, hold up a minute "I heard Roland say. I stopped at the bottom of the hill in Beachway. I believe the guy seeing me with the gun in hand as everyone else ran to grab their weapons. The guys went into the house. "Think they going to strap up "I said to Roland. "It doesn't matter because as soon as they come out, we are going to let them have it. "Kool-Aid said while checking the clip to his 45. As we all waited a guy came strolling into Beachway. "Man, that's the n***** that got me locked up and pointed me out to the police "Kool-Aid said as he ran over to the guy to get him across his forehead with his pistol. The guy went down holding his forehead as he was slowly getting up on his knees, I ran over kicked him square in the face knocking him back down flat. At that time the concrete in Caesar's Ford was all broken up. There were large pieces of black concrete. I started digging up large portions and dropping them on the guy's head. As I was picking up my third brick I was almost knocked down as a group of guys ran over and started kicking the guy as well. At first, I thought it was my homies but when I looked over my shoulder, I seen that it was the guys that had just served the junkie. They began stomping him while me and Kool-Aid kept dropping bricks on him. After a while Roland asked everyone to stop. We all backed away and noticed the guy wasn't moving. "Damn y'all killed the man "Ready said. One of the neighbors call the ambulance. Once we heard the sirens everyone dispersed but the guy still hadn't moved yet. I went and stood in the woods at the top of Beachway watching as the paramedics put him into the ambulance. One of the neighbors was talking to the paramedics while looking down at the victim on the stretcher. Finally, the ambulance pulled away, but the police stayed. They began asking the neighbors questions in which everyone claim to have seen nothing. After about an hour we were all back on the block but this time the new group of guys joined us. We talked with one another for about 30 minutes. We learned that some were from Chicago and that they actually hung out in Cedar Green Apartments. There was this one guy in particular who had a very strange voice. To me he sounded like a frog. Later I would learn his name was Bo skeet. After a couple days we were all chilling at the top of Beachway when some of the guys from Chicago came up to BOSKEE and gave him a weird handshake. Me and Ready ask them what it means. One guy started moving his fingers in the air like sign language. I burst out laughing asked him was he retarded or dancing. Everyone laughed. "Nah we Vice Lord's and Four Corners Hustlers," Boskee said to me. "What the hell is that" I asked. BOSKEE and the others started explaining things to us. Later a few of us was doing the same handshake it was more of a fad at first. I was still on the run when we first started claiming Vice Lords.

Chapter 9

Buying Crack

By me being on the run it was constantly making the block hot, so I called an old childhood friend who was from New York and went to Hidden Valley elementary School with me and told him I was on the run and needed to come lay my head for a while. Without question he told me to come on. I arrived in Belmont North Carolina in April 1993. My partner was living in a hotel with his girlfriend. He was only 15 but had two cars. At that age he was buying 2 oz of crack. Back in them days you could make $3,000 in breakdowns off each one. That's pretty good for 15-year-old. I stayed for a little while hustling out the hotel room. His mom and pops live a few rooms down and they both got high. His mom used to take me all over Belmont and Mount Holly North Carolina as her bodyguard. I must admit his mom was beautiful. She was very slick and knew the game well and taught me some of her experiences in life. After a couple of weeks of being there something had happened between a guy and my homie female cousin. I really don't remember what they were arguing about. I was chilling in the room watching TV when I heard the commotion. I hopped up off the bed and peek through the window curtain and seeing a guy arguing with my homie cousin. I continue to watch until the guy angrily jumped out the car I ran into the bathroom and grab my homeboy 22 semi-automatic rifle and ran straight towards the door. I snatched the door open and asked the guy what the f*** did he think he was doing. When the lady sees me with the gun, he told me to go back in the room. I ignored her and told the guy to get missing. He acts as if he wanted to protest but when I cocked it, he slid back into the car as he was backing up, I heard him say, "I'll be back" at that moment I've been getting to let off shots into the car as he was backing up. I found out later that the guy was struck in the jaw but survived. There was many shells laying on the ground and my homeboy cousin ran over to pick up all the shells "we got to get rid of the evidence" she said. "Well, you get rid of it I'm going back inside the room", I said. I went back into the room and sat back down on the bed and continue watching TV. "How can you be sitting down watching TV after what transpired" she asked me. I don't know if I was confident that the guy wouldn't tell or being only 14 years old, I didn't truly grasp the concept of how serious the situation was. Either case I wasn't bothered. I knew my prints wasn't on the casings. So, I told her she had to flush the casings down the toilet because her parents were on them now. Luckily the guy didn't die because there were a few witnesses that watch everything go down but what was even more shocking is that the police never came. Me and my homie from New

The Hidden Valley Kings

York used to drive back and forth from Belmont to Charlotte. We were both no older than 15 but he had the work so I used to move the packs for him and Belmont because he was hustling in Charlotte after I finish my pack; he would come pick me up and we will head back to Charlotte just to hang out and chill. The only thing I hate it about riding with him is that every time we headed back to Belmont it was always late and we were both High off weed and for whatever reason he always fell asleep behind the wheel some nights we will pull over and get shut eye for about 30 to 45 minutes. It wasn't long before I was locked up for murder. I would never forget that day everything seems so clear as if it happened a few hours ago. It was Easter Sunday 1993 and as usual I was sitting in the hotel watching television. My homie and his girl had gotten into an argument earlier that day. But after a few hours had went by they both had cooled off and was back hugging and kissing and playing. I remember sitting on the edge of the bed rolling a Philly blunt when they both came into the room. They both sat down on the other bed and was whispering and smiling to one another. I didn't think anything of it as I continued to finish rolling the blunt. My homie had a 22 revolver with a hair trigger. He pulled it out to show it to me and begin opening the chamber and spinning it before closing it back. He aimed a gun at his girlfriend in a playful manner and she kept telling him to stop playing with the gun before it goes off. I kept my eyes on the TV. As I begin pulling on the blunt and waiting for its affects to hit me, I heard the gun go off. I look to my right and see my homie reaching for his girl "oh s*** Monique "I heard him say. At first, she didn't make a sound or move in about 3 seconds she grabbed the side of her chest and started squirming calling out my homeboy's name. But here screaming didn't sound normal. It was a scream that let you know it was in pain. My homeboy wraps his arms around her screaming her name as well. I believe once it settled on him what had just taking place he jumped up and ran to his mom room across the parking lot to inform her what just happened. I looked down at his girlfriend as she laid stretch out on the bed with her eyes closed and her mouth open. She was no longer squirming. A loud snoring noise was coming from her opened mouth. I knew what the snoring meant but didn't know what to do to save her. So, I just stared and waited for help. About 3 minutes later my homie and his mom came through the door followed by others. Everyone stood around looking like the mom called the ambulance. After hanging up my homeboy mom came over with the others and looked down at her son's go girlfriend. "She goes be alright. She's just sleeping right now. Y'all hear her snowing don't you. Yea she goes be just fine". Everyone else agreed. I looked up in shock. I knew she wasn't alright. She wasn't snoring because she was sleepy, she was snoring because she was drowning in her blood. But I didn't bother to mention it. The ambulance pulled up along with police and we were all taken to the station for questioning. I gave them my older cousin's name because I was on the run. After the questioning everyone was release except me. They checked my hands for gun powder and then put the cuffs on me." What's going on" I asked. "You're under arrest" an officer replied. "Under arrest for what, I didn't do shit" "Well there are witnesses who claims otherwise". "Man, this some bullshit". "You are being charged with the murder of Monica Narrow." They led me from Belmont police station and drove me to Gastonia jail. I was placed in lock up waiting to see a judge. They thought I was sixteen because I gave them my cousin Andrew Malight name. Early the next morning I was taken back to Belmont police station. I was brought to the same integration room as the day before. " Why didn't you tell us your real name and that you were only fourteen?" "Huh??" I asked, "what you mean?" " Your mother and aunt spoke with us at 3:00am this morning. And you have a juvenile warrant in Charlotte." I didn't say nothing as they retook my fingerprints." "So, what I'm charged with now" I asked in hopes they were letting me go because I was a kid. " You're still being charged with murder but now it's accessory after the fact" a tall skinny white officer said. He chewed on his tobacco while he thumbed through some papers. An officer came and escorted me out the station and into a patrol car. "Were you taking me too?" I asked I'm driving you to the juvenile facility in Gastonia. As we drove to the detention center my mind drifted off. I was thinking about how Monique died. And as I was thinking about her, I began to think about the time I was shot. I believe I was only twelve. It was during the summer, and

90

The Hidden Valley Kings

I was standing in Hidden Valley Apartments sipping on some Madd Dog 2020. I was arguing with an older guy about who was the best player in the NBA between Michael Jordan and Magic Johnson. As I sipped me drank acting grown a car pulled up and two or three niggas hopped out. Everyone scattered. I didn't know the guys or had beef with them, but I did what everyone else did and I ran too. I headed towards the back of Hidden Valley Apartments. I came to a dead end with nowhere to go. I heard shooting and became desperate in getting away. But there was nowhere to go. I then noticed that some off the apartments were empty, so I started kicking at the back door of one of the apartments. I looked to my right and seen a tall chubby nigga with a 12-gauge coming my way. One last kick and the door flew open. At the same time the door was open I heard the shot but ran inside. I begin running for the front door, but my leg locked up on me and became stiff. After a few seconds my leg loosen back up and I made it out the front door. Soon as I hit the parking lot, I seen the guys jumping back in the car and sped off. I looked around to see if there were any casualties. Everyone looked ok. As I begin to walk across the parking lot my leg tightens up again and I started walking with a limp. One of the older homies noticed I was shot and threw me over his shoulders. Someone called the ambulance, but I refused to go to the hospital. Later I walked home with holes in my legs. Luckily, I was hit with buckshot's. I decided to walk home and when my mom seen the blood specs on my leg, she asked me what happened. "I got shot" I said, as I walk past her and into the house as if a twelve-year-old getting shot was normal. My mom panic and became hysterical. "I'm calling the ambulance" she said. "Somebody already did that, and I told them I didn't want to go" I said looking down at my leg. My mom called the ambulance anyway and I was taken to the hospital. I had about five or six holes in my leg. They treated me and sent me home. A few days later I was in Hidden Valley Apartments when an old head pulled up and ask if I had weed. I told him I didn't, but I knew where to get some. He told me to hop in the car so we could go see the weed man. Some hours later I ended up being in the car with three older guys. We drove around Charlotte for a while. I had no idea what they were planning. All I know is that we ended up in Grier Town and they robbed at least five people in Grier Town. Next, we headed to West Blvd. and the robbing continued. We ended up at a 7even eleven I sat on the parking lot. The older

homies started talking and planning to rob the store. One of the homies said he had to pee and went on side of the building. A few seconds later he called me over. I walked over to him. " What's up" I asked. "Man, we are getting the fuck up out of here" he said. " "Why what's up". " Them stupid niggas about to rob the store and it has cameras in it. They are going down and I'm not go let you get caught up in that." So, we ended up walking away and caught a ride to Wilmore and from there we caught a ride back to the Valley. I didn't see the old heads any more after that.

But I did learn after that that one of them ended up killing their own brother and set house on fire to cover it up.

Chapter 10

Detention

I snapped out of my daydream when I heard the officer say we here. Gaston Detention Center I was taken into the detention center and led to a small office. I was told what I was charged with and the facility was ran. After about 30 minutes I was moved to another part of the center and was given a shower. Once my shower was done, they put me in a single man cell. A white lady brought me my state issued clothes. I laid down on the bunk thinking about my family and the hood. I wondered what the homies was up to. I haven't seen them in a while, but I knew they was doing what we been doing s*** don't stop when a n***** get locked up. Around 5:00 pm my door was opened to go eat dinner. There were about 20 juveniles in the day room. I found a seat and sat down. After dinner we were allowed to go outside and play basketball. I didn't play for a couple of days because I was still feeling out my surroundings. Although I've been locked up before, this was a different city. I ended up becoming great friends with a guy who went by the last name Lemberger. He was a hell of a basketball player and I heard he could have made it pro, but he got hooked on drugs later on in life. He was out of Hickory North Carolina. And boy could he ball even at that young age of 15 he was indeed something special. A couple of days later my attorney came to visit. She explained to me my charges and also that Gaston County came with some new charges. They claimed that I sold to an undercover back in 1992. I was charged with two counts of selling to an undercover. She also told me that my homie was captured in New York and was waiting to be extradited back to the Carolina's. She also explained to me that the D.A. office wanted me to testify on my man. A week later I was in court for my hearing. The judge asked if I understood what I was being charged with and I told him yes, I did also the DA stood up and said that I was charged with another charge serving toward undercover. After my hearing I was led back to the holding cell to be transferred back to the juvenile Detention Center. I remained at the center until my next court date which was about a month later. My attorney came to visit me in the holding cell, and she told me that my homeboy was in court that day also. She explained to me that they wanted me to testify as to what happened with the shooting. "Wait a minute" I said, "I thought I was going to court today." I explained to her that I didn't want to testify and that I wasn't going to at that time an officer came to lead me into the courtroom. I saw my homeboy his mom and sister as they were leading me to the witness stand. Once I was seated the DA asked me my version of that day. I remain silent. The district attorney continues to ask me questions and I continue to remain silent. The judge didn't ask if I had anything to say I responded no, and my lawyer stood up and explained to the courts that I refuse to testify. As I was led back out of the courtroom my homeboy mom and sister smiled and waved at me, I smiled back and then I look back at my homeboy and he mouth the words thank you. I gave him a head nod as they led me back into the holding cell. My lawyer came to see me about 15 minutes later and she explained to me that the courts was going to bound me over to Superior Court for serving the undercover and that I would be charged and tried as an adult. "Can they do that" I asked. She said for me not to worry and that she was going to fight to keep the charge and juvenile court and that she would be out to see me at the center sometime next week. The day I went back to the center my probation officer from Charlotte came to visit me and explain to me that once my court hearings was over with, I will be transferred back to Charlotte to face another charge for probation violation. Once my probation officer left, I was able to go in the day room with the other juveniles. Everyone was asking me how court went, and I told them the situation and they responded by shaking their heads and saying good luck. I went to court again about 3 weeks later but this time it was in Superior Court, and I was being charged with selling to an undercover the district attorney offered me a plea saying that they will give me 3 years' probation if I play guilty to the drug charge. My attorney advised me not to take the plea and that she was going to fight to have my case sent back to juvenile court. But I told her that I wanted to go home and that if I play guilty would I be able to leave out today. She told me yes, I would be able to leave but that discharge may come back to haunt me later down the road. I wasn't trying to spend more weeks in the Detention Center I was just a kid and I want it out. I

asked her about the charge of accessory to the fact after murder and she said that charge was dropped but since I refuse to cooperate with the authorities, they decided to bound my juvenile charges over to adult charges. After me and my lawyer argued back and forth about my plea we went ahead and signed the plea. I was taken back to the center waiting to be transferred back to Charlotte which wasn't going to be until someone had to go to court, and they would take me then. That same day I seen two detectives come to the center and they were speaking with one of the staff members and I noticed they kept looking over at me they handed her some papers and then they left. I don't recall the lady's name, but she did ask me to step in her office and she began to explain that I was being charged with three counts of murder back in Charlotte and that the officers wanted to speak with me but by law they couldn't without my parents or lawyers' consent because I was a juvenile. "Man, I ain't killed nobody" I said to the staff. She replied, "I don't know if you did or if you didn't but what I do know is that these are very serious charges, and you are charged with them". "I need to speak with my lawyer" I said, and she gave me the phone. I explained to my lawyer what was going on and she told me not to speak with anybody and to sit tight until I was extradited back to Charlotte. SENT AWAY I arrived back in Charlotte sometime in May or June of 1993. I was taken to Gatlin juvenile facility in Huntersville North Carolina. I had to go through the usual screening such as showers, orientation etc. I was taken to my cell and was told that I had to do 24 hours in my cell before I was allowed to come out. The next day I went out into the day room. I see guys I went to school with and some I was beefing with on the streets. I had no problems there. My family came to see me. I explained toy father of the new charges that they were trying to hit me with. "Just stay strong and focused and no matter what, be a man about it" my father said. My mom kept smiling because she was happy to see me. She told me that Kool-Aid was shot in his arms the other day but that he was ok. I asked my dad what happened, and he told me that Kool-Aid and one of my other friend "Ike" got into an altercation and that Kool-Aid stabbed him in the arm. Ike responded by shooting Kool-Aid. I sat there trying to figure out what the hell is going on with my homies and why didn't anyone try and stop them fools. Family don't hurt family. We were Vice Lords and Lords don't put their hands on other Lords. My mom told me that my younger sisters miss me and that my baby sister Rosie always crying for me. After my visit I asked if I could go back to my cell. Once in my cell I laid down on my bunk looking up at the ceiling. My attorney came to visit me the next day. She explained to me about the murders. She said that I was not charged with the murders but that I was the number one suspect, but the police didn't have motive. So as of right now I wasn't charge with the three murders. I went out into the day room to watch the news. What's the news was over with I began listening to the radio that the staff kept inside a little room with chairs and a couch. A little while later my friend "Mali Boo" came to get me to play spades. "Mali Boo" was charged with several murders I think like four or five. He was too young to get the death penalty, so they were pushing to give him life. He told me how everything started from beginning to finish. Him and his codefendant "Booshay" were both at the juvenile Center. I've known both of them since knee high days. I remember Mali Boo telling me he wishes he could get the death penalty because he couldn't see himself spending the rest of his life in prison. He was only 15 years old, but he had an old soul. After playing cards it was time to lock into our cells. This is the time that I gather my thoughts. Laying on my bunk inside that cell I started reminiscing again.

I was 11 years old and me and Ready was out hunting. Hunting is when we go all over the neighborhood looking for outsiders that don't belong there. My older friend Hightower wanted to come along but we needed a ride. I told Ready to go and get a screwdriver in hammer so I can still the car. Hightower convinced us ride with his uncle. I thought this might not be a good idea considering the fact that we are about to do something criminal. Hightower said he was going to go get his uncle and that they both would pick us up so me and Ready waited on the corner of Springview and Wellingford slap boxing. A few moments later they pulled up and we both hopped in. I let Ready do the talking. Ready was able to convince Hightower uncle that we were just riding around to go see girls. We went on our mission cruising through the hood street by Street looking for victims. We pulled up on some guys that we didn't recognize it was about four or five of them. We told Hightower uncle to let us out and that we just passed the girls house, but we wanted to walk because we didn't want them to see us get dropped off. He said he understood and let us out further down the street. "Man, what's in that bag" Hightower uncle asked Ready as he was shutting the door. Ready ignored him. Me and Ready began walking back towards the group of guys. Hightower remained in the car with his uncle. Ready had a Mossberg pump and I had a revolver. "Check this out, "Ready said. "When we get up on these n***** ask one of them for a light and when he go in his pocket I up the pump" "man that s*** ain't going to work", I said. "What you mean it ain't going to work" Just like I said that s*** sounds stupid. Because for one that big ass gun they go see from a mile away" "Yeah you right.

Why don't you come up with something then n*****" "Okay check this out then. Why don't you put that pump inside your pants and when we get up there, I asked one of them if they got change for a ten dollar bill" "Man that's a dumb idea that s*** ain't going to work either because they're going to see me walking stiff leg" "Yeah you right" We were getting closer and had to come up with a plan quick. The victims were all standing around talking loudly and disrespecting one of our Valley girls. We were about 40 yd away and still had no idea how we were going to play this. Now we were about 15 yards up on them and I heard one of them say "yeah y'all Valley girls pretty and things but all y'all p**** stink why is that" "Yo mama p**** stank n*****"I heard the girl say. And all the guys burst out laughing. We were now 10 yards away and Ready still hadn't said anything about a plan this I already knew meant we were going to freestyle this one. My heart started beating fast and my dick was hard because I had to piss. This was that strong nervous piss. It was dark and no one had looked up yet to take notice of us. The hood was quiet and the only noise that could be heard was from these loud m************. A couple more feet closer and Ready up the pump. "Nobody moves" he said. All at once everyone started pleading and begging. I remember hearing words like "oh s***" "not again", "come on man" "you got it slick". The girl screamed. "Shut the f***** up " I said. She stopped screaming. "What street you live on" I asked. She told me her Street and I told her to go home. "Man, that b**** set us up" I heard one of the guys say. As they were going through their pockets and pulling out all their belongings, Kool-Aid pulled up. I had seen the car approaching while we had everyone at gunpoint but as long as it wasn't the police, I didn't give a f***. I kept one eye on the car and the other one on the n******. The car started slowing down but before it made a complete stop, I heard Kool-Aid voice scream from the driver side "what we got here". "We got it" Ready said. Kool-Aid started pulling off yeah through the window "I want those Bo Jackson's that n***** got on his feet" then pulled off. It all happened so fast. I see the n***** to my left make a sudden move but before I realize what he was doing he up what look like a 25 automatic. He aimed at me and fired. Luckily, he missed. Almost simultaneously Ready up his pump and fired at the guy. He missed too. Now everyone was scattering. The one guy was still shooting his 25 automatics. I let off two shots and ran behind a car that was parked on side of the road. I heard Ready shoot again. I knew it was him because that gauge was the loudest. At the same time, I was running behind the parked car I seen one of the guys run behind the tree, but he was bending down as he got close to the tree which indicated he had a gun stashed there. And I was right. He came up fast just as quick as he squatted and started shooting. It sounded like Vietnam in the Valley, as shots rained out through the quiet still noise of the neighborhood. The other guys jump in a car and pulled off. Me and Ready took off running in the opposite direction. As we got further down the street, I heard Ready say "damn!!" "What's wrong" I asked. "Man, I dropped the damn bag" The bag he was referring to be a black bag that he carried the pump in. We both knew we had to go back and grab that bag. Can't leave anything behind. We Begin jogging back to the scene I was a little nervous because I had only two shots left. But once we got to the area no one was in sight, but the bag laid on the ground and next to it was scatter pieces of some of the guy's belongings we grabbed those too and begin jogging again. Me and Ready ran in a straight line down the street. After about a quarter a mile I started getting tired and what's worse we could hear ambulance in the distance. As I begin slowing down Ready begin picking up his pace once we heard the sirens. "Man f*** this", I said in stop running. I began walking trying to catch my breath. I watched as Ready got further and further in distance. I fired up a Newport and continue walking but this time I was walking in the shadows of people yards. After walking past six seven houses I decided to jump someone's fence. After jumping 8 or 9 fences I ended up on the same street as red which was a coincidence. I began strolling through the front yard of the house whose backyard fence I had just jumped. Ready didn't notice my presence in the dark night because the front yard had no light therefore, I was in the shadows. "Ready" I called out He made a complete stop. "Niger where you at" he whispered. "I'm over here" I said Ready lean Forward with his chin sticking out moving his head trying to locate me. He started jogging my way. "Man, we hit somebody " Ready said. "Man, you hear them ambulance don't you" "I looked at Ready and said "that s*** don't mean it has anything to do with us that s*** could have happened

somewhere else" "Yeah right "Ready said, not believing me. We both ducked when we see a car creeping down the street. I ease the hammer back on my pistol and remain low. The car continued to creep at a mighty slow pace. As the car crept by us, we both recognize the car, it was HighTower and his uncle. We both ran out into the street screaming Hightower's name. The car slammed on brakes, me and Ready both made a run for the car. "Wait a minute where did you get that big ass gun from". Hightower uncle asked Ready. Me Ready and Hightower all look back and forth at each other. "Huh! what you say?" Ready responded trying to buy time think up something fast. "Where you get that big ass gun from, that's what I said" "Oh yeah my fault" "Was that y'all doing all that shooting" "Yeah but not really "Ready replied again. As we drove through the hood heading back to the block, Ready begin giving his version of the story. "You see, this the b******* that happened. We went to go see the girls, but they had some niggas over there, and we all got into an altercation. One of the guys had this gun and I took it from him when he tried to pull it on us" Amazingly the uncle believes the story. I don't remember what happened after. But I remember going over to Roland and Ready crib the next day and finding out that one of the guys was indeed shot and that they called the ambulance from a pay phone on Tom Hunter. Also, no one died. However, me and Ready was chastised by the older homies. They said that me and Ready were hard-headed and that we were renegades doing what we wanted to do and that we had to stop. Roland asks me what had happened. So, I explained the situation to all the guys. Ike asked me where the gun was at, and I told him I got rid of the gun because I didn't know if the guy was dead or not. This started an argument. Kool-Aid was pissed. He kept walking back and forth thumbing his nose. He looked at Roland and asked, " are we throwing away guns now". "Man, I told you why I did it "I said to Kool-Aid. Kool-Aid through his hands up in the air and said "f*** that all these guns done shot somebody we ain't been throwing guns away. If that's the case, we might as well throw all these m*********** away." "I ain't throwing s*** away "I heard Ready say. "Scoe do you know where you put the gun at" Ike asked. "Yeah, I know where it's at "I said. "We need to get that back" Me and Ready left together to go retrieve the gun.

I woke up the next morning and we all are lined up to eat breakfast. After breakfast we all went into the day room. I noticed about three or four guys huddled up in the corner whispering. I walk over to see what they were discussing. I stood to the side and overheard them discussing ways to break out.

Everyone in the group agreed to play they part and trying to escape. When they broke their huddle up, I pulled my man from North Charlotte to the side. He was in for murder also. I told him them n****** bluffing and that they were going to leave him out to dry. He told me two of them was from his hood and he trust them. I said nothing else about it. About 30 minutes later they called out the names of those who had to go to school. My name was one of those called and I left with everyone else heading towards the little classroom in the back. Everyone entered the classroom and found a seat.

No one was actually doing any work. Everyone was talking about their cases to sports to n***** in The Hood etc. I was chopping it up with a guy from New York who was telling me about a group called the 5%. As we continue talking, I noticed two or three of the guys who are huddled up in the day room where now huddled up in the classroom. I looked at my man from North Charlotte and shook my head and letting him know the people he thinks is going to ride with him is going to betray him. He gave me an agitated look and continue talking to the huddle up guys. My man from North Charlotte jumped up out of his chair and charge the teacher who is a staff and punched her in her face knocking her down he then ran out the classroom as if he was heading for the front entrance, he was tackled by two other staff members the other guys who was supposed to have his back stood still with their mouths open. Only one of them tried to do something but it wasn't much, all he did was pick up a chair and throw it against the wall and sat back down in another chair. It all happened so fast. I stood up to get a better view of what was taking place. The staff started running inside the classroom telling everyone to sit down and not to move. As I was standing up, I seen my man on the floor cuffed up with the whole left side of his face swollen. We looked at one another and I shook my head and mouth the words "I told you so". They locked us in our rooms until later that evening. That evening I kicked it with the guy from New York as he expounded on his definition of the five percenters. He gave me the supreme mathematics and alphabets. I looked over the papers that he had given me, and I started asking him questions but for some reason he couldn't answer not one single question. And with that I decided that the 5% is something I didn't want to be a part of. But the supreme mathematics in alphabets was very intriguing and I really wanted to know more but he wasn't the one to give it to me.

Chapter 11

Training School

I stopped praying to God a long time ago once I seen that none of my prayers were being answered and that it was chaos death and confusion all around me. Also, the way God was being explained to me started to not make sense at a very young age. I finally went to court for my probation violation, and I was sentenced to C.A. Dillon training school. Once I got back to the juvenile Center everyone was asking me what happened in court. I told them that the judge was sending me to C.A. Dillon training school, and everyone started moaning and sighing. "what's wrong" I asked. Everyone started telling me how f***** up that training school was and how rough it was and that I will be fighting every day. They said that the training school I was being sent to was considered maximum security for juveniles. This is where they send murderers who was too young to be sent to prison. I mentally prepared myself for what was about to come whatever it maybe I knew it wasn't a turning back once I enter inside that fence at the training school. I finally arrived at CA Dillon training school in Butner North Carolina in 1993. I was taking to B Cottage. There

108

were three cottages A B and C. A cottage was designated for the females, C cottage was designated for those convicted of sex crimes, and B cottage was for those who was charged with anything from murder robbery and multiple assaults. There was about six or seven of us that came together on the van. We were all sent to our individual cottage. Me and another guy who was at Gatlin Detention Center with me was sent to B cottage. Everyone else was sent to C cottage. Once I entered B cottage, I was told to go to wing one. Each cottage had three wings. They sent the guy who came with me to wing two. I was told that I would have to attend group meetings every week. Also, there was levels. These levels went to six. You had to start with zero points. After you reach a certain number of points, you graduate to the next level. These levels came with more privileges. This consisted of getting home passes, staying up late, using the snack and drink machine etc. I had to go through a two-week orientation. During that orientation I had to participate in group sessions. My first week there I got into a fight with a guy from Charlotte who got his head boost up from a guy from Winston-Salem. I don't even know what caused the fight. It was early in the morning, and I was leaving off Wing one to enter Wing 2 for the group session. When I walk through the door the guy stuck his hand out as if to greet me and then he swung. I immediately duck and grabbed him by his legs and then slammed him on the floor. Once I had him on the ground, I began punching him repeatedly in the

109

face. After about 20 or 30 seconds the staff broke us up and put us both in our rooms. I believe I remained in my cell for two days. While in my cell my mind drifted down memory lane. It was the fall of 1990. I was chilling on the corner of Welling Ford and Springview when I see my homie Keenan walking down Springview headed my way. "What you got going on" he asked. I was playing with a 22 Derringer that I had just got from a junkie. I showed him the 22 and he laughed asking what can you do with that? "The same thing I would do with any other gun " I said. He reached for the gun, and I gave it to him to check it out. We then headed to the corner store called the Galaxy. Once in the store Keenan bought a soda and why he was at the counter I was stuffing chips and a soda inside my pants and walk past him and the cashier outside. When Keenan stepped outside, I was eating a bag of chips a few seconds later the African cashier follow Keenan outside. "Little Roscoe, I seen you swipe those chips and soda I'm going to tell your mother and father the next time they come in my store "the African said. "Man, I ain't stole s*** out your store "I responded as me and Kenan began to walk off. We stood at the corner of North Tryon and Wellingford Street. There was a bank across the street in Tryon mall parking lot. Keenan began heading in that direction, so I followed. "what's up" I asked. "We finna get this money" he said. I didn't ask any questions I just continue to follow. We reached the bank which was only a few yards from where we were standing. "Okay look" he said. " We go rob the next person that come up to this machine" "Oh yeah s*** I'm with that" I said. We stood there for approximately 15 minutes before I victim pulled up. A black man stepped out of a white Jaguar and walked up to the machine. "Scoe hurry up and get up on him" Keenan said. I pulled out my 22 Derringer and began slowly walking up to the guy. As I got closer, I noticed the guy watch me at the corner of his eye. I continue to approach, and he continue to watch. As I got within four or five feet of him, I seen him brandish a chrome 357. But that wasn't about to stop me. And then I heard Keenan voice telling me to come here. I turned around and he was making facial expressions letting me know to let it go he had seen the gun as well. I look back at the dude contemplating. The dude now had the gun at waist level pointing directly at me. "Damn" I thought to myself Keenan f***** up the lick. My young mind actually believe I could have pulled it off. We left the bank and headed towards Club Expressions on North Tryon. As we got closer to the club Keenan asked for the 22. He then started walking towards a guy that was about to get in his car. I began to follow. " Nah stay back so we want to make him suspicious" Keenan said. I fell back a little and watched as Keenan approached the man. I really couldn't see what was going on. I see the guy pause to see what Keenan wanted. In seconds the guy and Keenan began tussling. I ran over to help but the guy was strong. I see a beer bottle leaned up against the building. I quickly ran over a grabbed it. I headed back towards the struggle. They both was fighting over the gun. I swung the bottle upside the guy head which caused him to buckle a little. I don't know who had control over the gun, but I do know the gun had failed to the ground in which I quickly picked it up. As the guy was trying to gain his composure from the blow Keenan slammed him up against the car and they begin tussling again. The guy slammed Keenan on his back and he fell on him. As the guy was getting up, I aimed the gun at him he put both hands up. I aimed a gun at his face and pulled the trigger. It sounded like a firecracker. The guy turned his face to the side grabbing it with both hands. As he began running, I heard him scream out "he shot me in my face "I aimed the gun at his back as he was running with his hands still covering his face and pull the trigger. I don't know if I hit him or not as the guy ran across North Tryon Street. I looked over at Keenan and he was laughing saying "boy we got to go "we took off running down Hershey Street in the hood which was located behind the club. I was released from Lock up and allowed to go into the day room with the other juveniles however I couldn't leave the building for 2 weeks. Anytime you got in trouble you had to stay on your wing for two weeks. I spent my two weeks' time watching TV. We used to watch Soul Train every Saturday. We really watch it do lust off the women. Soul Train was the highlight of the week. For those two weeks I wasn't allowed to leave and go anywhere, including the cafeteria. They brought me my food. Sitting in the day room waiting on my time to be up, befriended a couple of guys. My closest road dog Was a guy named Darrion Hicks. He was from Earl Village projects in Charlotte North Carolina. We became close. I had others I was cool with from Durham, Raleigh, Winston-Salem, and Fayetteville North Carolina.

After my time was up, I was allowed to participate in the everyday functions. This included going to the cafeteria, recreation, school etc. The food wasn't that bad neither. They served everything from grits and eggs to pork chops and burgers. They dessert was my favorite. They always served pies, cakes, and brownies. One day while eating in the cafeteria I got into an altercation. I was sitting at the table talking to another guy when some brushed up against me with saying excuse me. "Mother fucker! You better say excuse me" I said standing up and putting baser in my voice than necessary. The guy spun around. "Say what" he asked. "Nigga U heard me" " What's up" "What's up" I said getting into position. He got into position by grabbing both pants legs in the thigh area with one foot behind the other. He swung and I ducked grabbing both legs and scooping him up off his feet. The scoop was my favorite move. Because once I get my victim on the ground I began pounding right away. And that's what I was doing to this guy at the very moment. We were pulled apart by staff. Again, I had to go through the procedure of being locked in my room and not having any privileges. I liked the training school a lot better than the detention center. I had a little more freedom. We had a swimming pool that we

113

used during the summer. Sometimes even in the winter. We had a basketball team that played other training schools that came out to play. They traveled from different cities across North Carolina. We also had a pretty good library. Everything was done with the female juveniles. We ate together, went to school together, went to recreation together etc. I always wanted to go to the dances. The dances were everyone favorite. The dance was always on a Friday night. The male and female dressed in their best clothes. In order to participate in the dances, you had to go infraction free for a week. This was impossible for me to do for about a year. I was always getting infractions. I became close to a guy named Ron-Ron who had a cousin named CB. They were both from Earl Village. Ron-Ron is locked up somewhere for murder. But I remember one day we had gotten to an altercation with the guys from D Cottage. I really don't know what caused it. I remember Ron-Ron telling me that it was going down at school. I told Ron-Ron that I was skipping this go round because I've never been to the school dance, and I was determined to make it. The first couple of days didn't nothing happen. But the following day it popped off.

We were in class goofing around when Ron-Ron told me that it would be today. He said he was going chill with me so we can go to the dance and not get involved. About fifteen minutes later we heard a lot of commotion in the hallway and some of the girls ran inside the classroom screaming

114

(they are fighting, they are fighting) Ron-Ron jumped up and ran out the classroom. (Ron-Ron chill!!) I yelled out. But he went anyway. (Damn! Don't look like I'm going to the dance) I said to myself and ran out behind my nigga. Once I got in the hallway, I seen Ron-Ron fighting and getting down with two guys. I immediately ran to them and swung on one of the guys and the rumble was on. Everyone was fighting at the same time. I was pissed because my homie got involved after we had agreed to stay out of it. But now wasn't the time to bitch about it. I continued throwing blows nonstop. The guy finally backed me up to the railing on to off the steps. He grabbed my legs and began lifting me up trying to throw me over. It was about a 15-foot drop. I was up on the rail about to be tossed over when Ron-Ron ran over and saved me. The fight lasted about ten minutes. I was snatched up by a staff member who tried to get a little rough. This caused me to begin assaulting that staff. I was restrained by other staff members. This one staff grabbed my wrist from the back and bent it back. The pain was unbelievable. I was taken to my room and locked down. They were bringing others in as well. Everyone who was involved was locked down. I don't remember how long we were down, but I do know I was screaming at Ron-Ron for days about missing my chance to make it to the dance. He started laughing saying" nigga you ain't never been to the dance what makes you think it was going to be any different". He was right! I kept fucking up after fuck ups. It seemed that shit just

115

wouldn't go right. My mom should've named me Can't Get Right. After a week or so we were let out our rooms and allowed to go in the day room. Everything went pretty smooth for a while until me and this guy from Greensboro got into it. I forgot what it was about, but I do remember us agreeing to go in the bathroom and get it in. I had a total of about eleven fights in an 18-month period.

Chapter 12

Issues & More Issues

I first started my course on reading back when I was in the group home and picked up the book on Malcom X. However, it was a librarian at the facility I was at that sparked me to really take it seriously. Actually, there was a couple of staff members that snuck me many books to read.

However, it was the librarian who took special interest in me. She strongly believed in me and my abilities to be a great leader. After about a year they moved the girls to another facility and made C.A. Dillon an all-boys camp. Once the girls were shipped off it seems as if violence was at an all-time high. The girls kept some of us calm so that we can see each other. But that was now over with. Riots was more frequently. Riot It was the fall of 1994. I don't remember exactly what caused it. But if my memory serves correctly, it was on a day that Soul Train came on.

There was an issue with some of the guys on wing one. If I'm not mistaken, a staff member disrespectfully turned off the TV while the guys were watching Soul Train. One of the guys from Winston-Salem yelled over to our wing telling us what happened. Another guy on my wing from Durham to him that if it was him, he wouldn't go out like that. And told him they should handle their business. The guy from Winston-Salem began bobbing his head up and down as if getting hyped. One of the guys broke the TV by beating it with a table leg that he broke from the table. Moments later a staff member entered the wing and demanded the guy turn over the weapon. Everyone on our wing walked over to the window. We all stood and watched as everyone on wing 3 began to approach the staff member. They tried to circle him, but the staff member ran off the wing and quickly locked the door to the wing. We all stood there laughing. About a minute later he came back with another staff and they entered wing three. As I continued to look, I noticed the staff members started backing up to the door. In a split second all hell broke loose. I see everyone on wing three attack the staff. After about a minute a few of the guys ran off the wing and into the day area. They began destroying property. We were locked on our wing and couldn't get out, so we started destroying the property on our wing. Through all the commotion I decided that this was the perfect time to get this guy who was talking shit the day before. I charged him swinging. We tussled until we were tired. After we realized that neither of us could go on fighting, we turned our attention to the facility and started destroying its property. The riot lasted for a long time until the local police and firemen showed up. They went to each wing knocking down and cuffing brothers. It was pretty easy since all the inmates were locked on their wings which means we were already somewhat detained. Our wing was the last wing they hit. The firemen came through the door with the water hose and started spraying everybody.

Some of us ran to the back and braced ourselves. The water was powerful and was knocking people across the room. I grabbed my mattress off my bunk and folded it. When the police and firemen came my way, I put my back against the wall and held my mattress up as a shield. The hose was so powerful that the water threw me up against the wall and I bounced off onto the floor. Officers rushed over and grabbed me. They held me down as I was being handcuffed. I was kicking and biting to no avail. Once I was finally cuffed, I was thrown into my cell with the cuffs still on. It took another 15 minutes for the facility got control. We were all put on lockdown in A cottage. I don't remember how long we were down, but I do know that the administration lied to the news saying we were only down for a couple of days. This was far from the truth. We were down some weeks and even went to court while we were down. After about a week or two we all decided to try and break out. I don't know whose idea it was, but everyone was on board, we just needed a plan. The Escape attempt One day while laying on my bunk and listening to Jodeci I thought I heard someone banging on my wall. I snatched my headphones off to make sure. It was my neighbor trying to get my attention. "Yooo!" I yelled out. "BJ want you!" My neighbor screamed back. I eased off my bunk and headed to the door. "What up BJ" "Shiiiid, nothing much. What u doing in there" "I was listening to my headphones dreaming about the streets." I spoke. "Yeah, I know what you mean" BJ began beating on the door and rapping a Tupac song. After a few seconds BJ had damn near our whole wing rapping along. Niggas began rapping other songs "Straight Out of Compton and "Fuck the Police" by legendary rap group N.W.A. "Hootie Hoo" by Out Kast. After numerous different songs the fellas was hyped and pumped up. We began talking about how much work we put in on the streets. " Man, just imagine if we all linked up as a force. We would be unstoppable!" said BJ. Everyone agreed. As we continued to kick it throughout the night someone came up with the idea of breaking out. It started off as just talk but as we continue to come up with clever ideas, it became serious. We all agreed that we had to get the keys somehow. I volunteered to get the keys. However, we were locked down which means it was going to be very hard to pull this shit off. I laid down on my bunk trying to figure this out. The guys continued talking with excitement. After a while I came up with an idea. I ran to my cell door. " A listen up y'all, I think I have an idea" I began to break down my plan. "Look!" I spoke. "We know the nurse comes to everyone cell door in the morning to check on us. She even opens the cell door to give us whatever is needed. I'm go request for a Tylenol and when she opens the door, I'm going to grab them keys." Everyone got quiet. After about 2 minutes BJ yelled out. " Shit let's see if it works." I told the guy across from me that I'm going to open his cell first and for him to get the key and open up the other cells as I try and fight off the staff if they come. Also, everyone whose door is opened must join me in fighting off the staff. Everyone agreed. A couple of days later I heard the nurse come in. "Nurse"! I heard her yell out. I jumped up, heart racing and nervous as hell. I walked to my cell door. The nurse went cell to cell. She opened the cell door to give the inmates their medicine. As I heard her getting closer to my door, the butterflies in my stomach were doing the most. I was nervous as hell. When I get butterflies and have to piss, it means I'm going to carry out whatever I'm planning. The nurse stopped at my door. "How are you this morning Mr. Abell." she asked. "I'm not doing too well". "Well, what's wrong son." "I have a cold and a headache"." I got something for you" she said. She reached into her bag and pulled out a bottle of pills. I braced myself ready to charge. She pulled out her keys and was about to open my cell door when I heard her say " oh!" As if she remembered something. She put the key up and bent down to slide me the pills under the door. I reached down to grab the medicine. "Have a nice day" I heard the nurse say, and she left the wing. "DAMN!!" I yelled out. "Man, I thought she was going to open the door" BJ said. "Yea me too, especially when she pulled the key out" I heard someone say. I walked to my bunk and sat down. "I can't believe that shit ain't work" I said to myself with my head down. "Why she opened the other cells but not mine?" I continued to stare at the floor. "We got to come up with another plan" I heard Black T call out. "Yea, cause that shit didn't work" another voice replied. I continue to stare at the floor trying to gather my thoughts. "Yo Scoe what's the game plan my nigga" BJ called out. "Shiid I don't know" I yelled back. Everyone got quiet and it was pretty much like that the rest of the day. Everyone was disappointed that my game plan didn't work and the excitement of actually escaping and not being able to, pretty much drain every one of their excitement as we were forced to face reality that we were not going to get out and so, everyone was lost in their own thoughts. Second escape attempt A few days went by and again we trying to figure out a game plan that might work. One night a guy named RB yelled out " aye yo! I just bust my light and guess what? It looks like I can crawl through it." "Man, what are you talking about" BJ yelled back. "Man, I broke my light, and I can see straight through it and it looks like it leads into the hallway. The lights in our cells hung on the wall just above the sink. It was a big light with a gigantic covering that was in a box shape. It's big enough for someone to crawl through. " So, you can get into the hallway?" I asked. "Hell yeah!"

RB said. "And you sure?" "Man!! Yeah!

Damn!" TM decided to try and break through his light to see if it was true. You could hear him banging on the light. As we continued to kick the bull shit, TM yelled out that his light was also finally ripped off and that he could see that it leads into the hallway. We started planning again. As I stood in my door looking out the window, I could see TM working his way through the ceiling to come out into the hallway. RB was doing the same thing. As I remain at my window, I seen the ceiling come crumpling down. I looked up and seen TM hanging from a large metal pipe. At that moment, the first door was opened. This we knew was a staff member doing their rounds. Before the staff reached the second door, TM climbed back into his room. The staff opened the second door and stepped onto floor. It was Mr. R. He paused for a second looking down at the debris.

Then he looked up at the ceiling. My heart was racing. I just knew our escape plot was over before we started. Mr. R. continued to look up at the ceiling as if he was trying to figure what happened. Amazingly he shook his head and started his rounds. After a couple of minutes Mr. R came back down the hall and stepped over the debris and went back through the door and locked it. Once we heard the door lock BJ asked TM what he was go do. TM responded by saying I'm climbing through the ceiling now. I stood at my cell door watching TM swinging from a large metal pipe. He let go and dropped down into the hallway. He jogged to the back of the hall and hid in the mop closet. Whenever a staff member come on the floor, they have to push a time clock to prove they did their rounds. Once TM was in the mop room, everyone got quite and waited. About an hour later a lady staff came on the floor and started her rounds. She walked towards the back and into the mop closet. I heard TM say boo!! The lady gasped at first. "Damn you scared me" she said. But then I guess it dawned on her that an inmate was out his cell because she started screaming from the top of her lungs. She took off running and I heard TM yell " come here bitch!!" The lady ran pasty cell door and off the floor. I see TM running behind her. "Damn! How the fuck did he fuck this up" I said to myself. A few seconds later TM ran back past my cell and into the mop room. Two male staff was running behind him. TM came out the closet with a mop ranger. There was a standoff between him and two black staff members. One of the staff members pulled out a pocketknife and him and TM was trying to figure out how to strike the other first. The staff member tried to rush in with the knife and TM swung the hell out that wrangler hitting the staff across the head. Blood sprayed the wall. We all began cheering. The staff stumbled a little. TM raised his weapon again and was about to swing when the other staff member tackled him to the floor. As the other staff member was trying to refocus, he stumbled over to try and help restrain TM. TM continued to struggle to no avail.

Finally, they were able to cuff him and pull him to his feet. I noticed a lot of blood on TM but thought it was the blood from the staff he had struck. We later learned that the staff member had actually stabbed him. They took TM off the wing floor and walked him off the floor. We all stood at our cell doors, again disappointed that our escape attempt failed. No one seen or heard from TM all night. We were wondering what could have happened to him. After a couple of hours, I laid down. The next morning, I heard the door unlock to the front entrance of the wing floor. I immediately jumped up and ran to the door. I heard TM yelling and cursing as he was being led back to his cell. After the staffs left, someone called out to TM. TM began explaining what happened after he was taken out. He told us that they hand cuffed him to the tv rail and beat him all night. He said they slapped him across the face all the way to the nurse station. "Man, what the fuck was you thinking when you said boo to the bitch?" asked K.W. "Man I don't know. I thought it was funny". We continued to listen to TM story on how the staff beat him. I believe a few days later we were all taken to court for our first appearance on the riot charge. I can only remember going to court one time. So, on that day I believe everyone entered a guilty plea. It was early morning when a staff member came on the floor and hollered for us to get ready for court. I jumped out my bed and ran to the cell door. I couldn't see which staff member it was, but knew it was a lady. A few hours later we were all being loaded into two white vans.

While getting into the van, one of the police officers dropped his cuff key. RB snatched it up as fast as it hit the ground. Once we were on the vans, they began searching everybody. RB stuck the key in his mouth. They made us all open our mouths after we were searched. When they got to RB, I was a little concerned. He opened his mouth and the officer made him move his tongue around.

They found no cuff key. After searching everyone they gave up and the vans began to head out." What you do with the key" I asked. RB smiled and I could see the cuff key between his teeth. " How the hell you do that" RB smiled and said "I swallowed the key and held it in my throat.

After they searched my mouth, I swallowed it back up". I shook my head grinning. The bus ride to the courthouse was about forty-five minutes. We were taken inside and placed inside a holding cell. There was about a good thirty-six of us all cramped inside this little ass room. We began plotting our escape again since RB had the cuff key. Again, the plan was to go to Durham N.C. as a crew and take over. BJ was from a project call Few Gardens and another called McDoodle. They took a few of us into the courtroom. I was with the first group. I pled guilty to three years. I was charged with destruction of state property. I believe three accounts. The judge was a baldheaded white guy who never looked directly at me. He kept his head down the entire time. When we were brought back to our holding cells, the put me and the first group into another cell. They then took the second group. As we waited in the holding cell, a debate came up. The debate was, could Mike Tyson beat Hulk Hogan. I was going with iron Mike. Another kid disagreed, and we started arguing. The argument became heated, and we began fighting. We both had shackles on our feet, so the fight was a bit awkward. But nonetheless, we fought. After a minute or so, the deputy came up stairs and said that if we didn't knock it off, the judge was going to give us more time. They ended up taking the kid out the cell and put him back into the first cell. They brought the other half of the group back from court and put them in their holding cell. I was a little upset because RB had the cuff key but was in the other cell. After about an hour, we were all asked to get ready to head towards the van. The staff came and began calling out our last names to get on the van. Since my last name Abell, I was the first to get on. As I sat on the van, I watched everyone come out one by one in a single file line. I watched as RB bent down as if to adjust his shackles. I knew this was the moment where all hell was about to break loose. As RB stood up, I could see that the shackles were off. In that split second of me noticing this, RB took off running. "He's running he's running" one of the lady staff yelled out. Three police officers gave chase. As they were chasing RB, I heard the same lady yell "there goes another one!" I looked in the direction of her voice and seen DB running in the opposite direction. I began clapping and cheering them on. Although I wasn't able to get my chance to escape, It felt good to see someone else getting away. I watched everything from inside the van. Everyone was hollering and hooting. The excitement didn't last that long. RB and DB was captured within minutes. I see defeat in my Lil homie face. When they put RB into the van, he looked at me with a grin and said, " I was almost free". After settling in he finally told me how they were caught. RB said that he had actually gotten away, but when he looked back, he seen three officers wrestling DB to the ground, so he ran back to help and was taken down as well. After a couple of days, we were allowed to come out of our rooms. More juveniles had arrived by the time we got off lockdown. I noticed a few new faces.

Chapter 13

Copperhead Snake

After I was sentenced, I began to study the Satanic Bible written by Anton Levey. This book was very interesting. I learned so called spells and rituals that summoned demons. I was a kid, and this shit was fascinating. I wondered if the shit was real, so I took the next step, prayed to the devil, and asked him to reveal himself. He came to me in a dream. In my dream, I was sitting down by the pond looking out at the water. As I was sitting, an old man dressed as a priest came and sat next to me. He wore a black fedora, and his shoes and suit were black as well. I didn't say anything to him at first. I continued to stare at the water in silence. After a moment the old man spoke. "My son I'm here". I turned to look at him. "Who the fuck is you?" I asked. He smiled and said" my son, it is I, your father. Don't you remember? You asked me to reveal myself". At that moment he turned into a black copperhead snake. The snake was as round as the Yankees Stadium and its length had no ending. Its head was the moon. And when it opened its mouth, you could see hell. It smiled at me. That smile was at least 400 feet long. It towered over me. And then it spoke." I have given

129

you a gift. But it's up to you to figure out what that gift is. Once you discover it, you will be remembered forever" and then it turned into a black Raven and flew away. When I woke up, my radio was playing Satan by R Kelly. This blew my mind. As soon as my door was opened, I gave the bible back to the staff member who gave it to me. "I'm not fucking with that" I said. I then began to explain to him about the dream. He looked at me as if I was a ghost. He took the bible and said, " I need to speak with you more about your dream later on." He whispered. As he walked away, he looked over his shoulder and said "you right, you don't need the book. It's already in you, all you had to do was knock, and you've done that". My body shivered as I headed back to my room. Everything was cool as the months rolled by. I somehow stayed out of trouble. I believe it was my reading. Once I started reading I kind of liked it. But I didn't fall in love with reading until years later. In the summer of 1994, Ready and his training school came to play us. All the training school had basketball teams and they would travel to other training school to compete. But C.A. Dillon was not allowed to travel because we were considered maximum security, so everyone had to come to us and play. Ready came over to me and we chopped it up. He told me about the transitioning from Vice Lords to Queen City Kings. He explained to me why we were no longer VL's and that everyone who heard about me wanted to meet me. We talked about our homie Kool Aid who died on June 28th, 1993. Apparently, Kool Aid had a gun that Fruit took the bullets out of and once Kool Aid noticed the chamber was empty, he reloaded it up. Later on, he and Fruit was playing around, and Fruit grabbed the gun and pointed it at him. "N*** I'll shoot you" Fruit said in a playful manner. Kool Aid calling his bluff said, " pull the trigger n***" Fruit, thinking the gun was empty, pulled the trigger striking Kool Aid in the face. Kool Aid stumbled forward and began swinging on fruit. He died seconds later. This crushed our circle. To lose a homie and not be able to retaliate is pain beyond measures. They both were our friends, and the shooting was accidental. However, it still didn't change the fact that we lost a good one. Kool Aid mom wrote me from time to time and I knew by her letters she was hurting. Ready ran down to me on why we became Kings and who was who. He told me that the day it changed from Vice Lords to Kings I was included. I wasn't there physically because I was doing time for putting in work for the Hood so once the transition was made, I was in the books. He told me that Korn was the King of Kings and that he appointed two O.K.'s to every hood. There were four original hoods. Me and Ready talked for a while until it was time for them to leave. It wasn't long after that I was shipped off to start my prison sentence. I was charged as an adult and given 3 years. I was first sent to another training school called Dobbs where I remained for about two weeks. I was then taken to a county jail and stayed there for about two days. But within those two days I heard a white guy being pressured for sex by a couple more guys. After about an hour the white guy gave in and I had to listen to that shit all night. I was now seventeen and was headed to Morganton High Rise.

Morganton was a youth spread and was considered the worst of the worst. I was put on a bus and was headed to the youth spread. Morganton Highrise, I arrived at Morganton in the spring of 1995. The bus pulled up to a tall building with about sixteen floors. They took us prisoners into what looked like a warehouse. Inside we were greeted by the laundry workers who were also prisoners. The first person I recognized was New York. It had been years since I've seen him.

New York had gained some weight and appeared to have aged. (What's up man, what you do to get here?) He asked. While we waited for our supplies, I told him about the riot. After a few minutes into the conversation, we were asked to move along. We were given our showers and told to get dressed. We headed upstairs on the elevator. I was taken to the 12th floor and was met by a big healthy white woman. She was very disrespectful and had a crew cut. She sent me to my cell. I walked into my cell. I was placed on a 23-hour lockdown, only allowed to come out for showers and about 30 minutes to watch TV. The room was so hot that I use to walk around naked. The walls were always sweating, and they had only one big fan that was at the top of the hallway that was supposed to keep the prisoners cool. It didn't work. I had to pour water all over my body in hopes that it would help. We were allowed out our cells twice a day. So, if you had to piss, you would have to use empty soda bottles. I kept about four or five bottles. It was at Morganton Highrise that my studying of the Five Percent Nation became serious. I was given what you would call an enlightened. An "enlightener" was someone who was skilled in the lessons of the Five Percent. Once you completed all the questions and answers it was said that you are qualified to teach. However, many who thought they were qualified actually wasn't. Have to be mindful that we were all children from the ages of thirteen to twenty. The first lesson I was given was the Supreme Mathematics. The Supreme Mathematics was developed by Abu Shaheed and Clarence 13 X. (Clarence 13 X was the founder of the Five Percent Nation in 1964). The Supreme Mathematics consisted of a numerology from one to zero. One being Knowledge and zero being cipher. I had to learn this lesson verbatim. After completion of the mathematics, I was given the Supreme Alphabets which I had to learn verbatim as well. In fact, all of the lessons were to know verbatim. There existed eight lessons in total which was called the one-twenty. The one-twenty consisted of 1. Supreme Mathematics 2. Supreme Alphabets 3. 1-10 4. 1-14 5. 1-36 6. 1-40 7. Actual Facts 8. Solar Facts All the above was to be learned verbatim. Also, there was what we called plus lessons. These lessons were written by advanced members who understood the degrees. These lessons helped others to understand the eight. There also existed what is called the Universal Flag that was designed by the God Shammgod. The Universal Flag was made up of the Sun, moon, and stars. The Sun represents the Blackman, Moon represents the black woman, and the star represent the black child. The Flag has eight points which represents the eight rays of the sun as well as the eight lessons. The Universal

Flag also represented other things like the clouds of deception etc. A guard by the Mrs. M was considered an asshole and all the prisoners avoided her nasty attitude. She was very disrespectful. One day I was let out my cell for thirty minutes and me and Mrs. M got into a heated argument. She tried to scare me with her tactics. When she realized that I was definitely a different breed we somewhat became cool. Actually, it was Mrs. M who taught me how to shave. After a month or so I was moved into the day room with the other prisoners. Everyone wanted to sleep in the day room because we had more freedom and privileges. We were rarely locked down. We were allowed to go to canteen without being escorted by a guard. Those who wish to go to canteen had to get on the elevator. The elevator was where everything went down. Guys got jumped and robbed on the elevators. The elevators had cameras, but the prisoners would take their folder and cover up the camera when it was about to go down. The folders told other guards your custody level by the colors on your folder. All day you could hear commotion on the elevator as it passed your floor, and you will hear the elevator stop and guards rushing in with pepper spray. There was a war going on between the Five Percenters and the Gangster Disciples. The Crips and GDs had an alliance against the GODS. This war would go on for years to come. I enjoyed sleeping in the day room, but it was short lived. I forget the reason, but I was taken out the day room and was placed back in lockup. After about two months I made honor grade. Honor grade meant you was allowed to go out back. This is when they change you out of your brown uniform khakis and into green uniform khakis. You were then sent out back where you have lots of freedom. I've heard stories about going out back. It was rumored amongst the GODS that all the GODS out back was considered the elites among the Five Percenters. A guard came to my cell one morning and told me to get ready because I was going out back to honor grade. I was in shock. Actually, the whole tier was. "Man, how you go out back? You been in more shit than us." The God True Born asked. "I don't know God, bit I'm going" I said. It was true I was involved in any and everything the GODS was involved in. The only difference is I never got caught. The officer came and got me to take me out back. There was about nine more people on the floor going as well. The elevator stopped at all the floors to fit as many people in as possible. They let us off and went back to get others.

Chapter 14

5ᵗʰ Floor

They stopped on the 5th floor as well. The 5th floor is where the juvenile lifers were. My man Malibu was on this floor as well but unfortunately, he wasn't coming. We were taken out back and I was assigned to what I think was called Blue Ridge dorm. OUT BACK Once in the dorm I was approach by a GD who wanted to know if I ran with anybody. I told him I was GOD and a GOD by the name of Divine overheard me and embraced me. "Peace God!" He greeted me. "Peace!" I responded. "How long you've had knowledge of self? "Almost two years" I said. He asked me to follow him, and I did. We stopped at a bunk and he told me this is where I will be sleeping. I threw my bedroll on top of my bunk and began to observe my surroundings. I noticed there was actually two sides to the dorm. Guys were sitting around playing cards at the table or on their bunks. Everyone was moving at a fast paste. The noise was unbearable, dudes were in serious arguments on the verge of fighting, I seen guys trying to break in someone's locker. There was complete chaos. I loved it. As I was putting my things up and straightening my bed, the God

Devine approach with two other guys. "Peace God!" He spoke. "This here is the God Wise and the God Understanding." We all greeted in Peace. They began to give me the rundown on the environment and how the Gods move. After we had small talk we headed outside. It was then I was introduced to other Gods. Every day after dinner we had a mandatory cipher. A cipher is a circle of Gods. The circle represents 360 degrees. This is where the Gods build. Meaning breaking down the lessons in a scientific method as well as through mathematics. There was about sixty to seventy God's out back. There was God's from all over North Carolina. When I first went to the cipher the Gods sounded like scientists. However, none of us truly understood the lessons. Got to remember, we were all kids. But it sounded good though. Everything was cool for the moment. My man High Times came as well as my man Shawn. Shawn was Paco's older brother. I used to hustle with him back in the early 90's. High Times and Shawn didn't stay long and was shipped out because they were of age. After you turned 21 you were transferred to an adult prison. Some people were shipped off at the age of 18. In fact, I was scheduled to be sent to Foothills correctional. But I was released before it could happen. I spoke with my man Ready frequently over the phone. He had gotten out from training school and was doing his thing. He was out on bond after a guy tried to set him up with 9 ounces of coke. Ready went to meet this guy in Rockingham, N.C. They were coming from New York and was busted before he could reach

Ready in Rockingham. The police then tried to flip the guy. They were successful. The guy was to continue with the trafficking and set Ready up as well. When Ready met the guy, he was acting kind of wired which alarmed Ready. When Ready got out of his car and into the connect car he noticed that he was sweating. Ready not knowing what's going started watching everything around him. The guy handed Ready the coke and tapped the brakes three times.

Ready noticed it. "Hold on, I'll be back, I got to go grab the money." Ready said. Ready left the cocaine in the car and began walking towards his own car and that's when several police cars swarmed in and arrested Ready and his connect. Ready baby mom's mom put her house up to bond him out. Ready would later plead to a lesser charge because they never caught him with the drugs. The only thing they had on tape was Ready saying he'll be back. He had to serve about two years.

Out back had four dorms. I don't remember the names of the dorm because it's been about twenty six years since then. Two of the dorms were for people who worked off the prison grounds. It was these prisoners who snuck the cigarettes back in and sold them to other prisoners. We were allowed to go to commissary whenever we felt like it as long as the prison yard was open. In the summertime I use to go grab me an ice cream two or three times a day. It wasn't long before they took me out of Blue Ridge dorm and put me into another dorm. This dorm was one of the wild ones. Plus, there was a lot of GODS in there. Every day we hung together and moved in packs. You will see GODS in groups of seven walking to and from. We were the deepest throughout the state prison system. When the Five Percenters hit the Carolinas in the late 80's there was only one God, I can think of who helped it grow over time. By the early 90's the Carolinas was flooded. Especially since all the hot rappers were members.

AZ, Wutang Clan, Busta Rhymes, Rah Diggah, etc. and the list goes on. After I was placed into my new dorm I was assigned to another bunk and the Gods in that dorm greeted me with peace. Me and another God became close. He was from Greensboro North Carolina, and he went by the name "True King". That was my ace. There was another God who also hung with us. And the three of remained close. We stayed studying our lessons and building with other Gods to get better understanding of the literature. I had a few skirmishes while at Morganton, but nothing to serious. One fight I had was with a guy from Raleigh North Carolina. I don't recall what the fight was about, but it lasted about two minutes. We were located in the back of the dorm on the rec yard. This is where all the fights went down. It was hard for the C.O. to catch you. I remember him swinging on me first and we went at it. My man High Times ran over but I told him " I got

139

this" High Times backed up and said, " well handle your business" and my business I did handle. But I didn't beat the guy down because he was a fighter and I believe if the fight went a lil longer he would have won because I was tiring out. But luckily, I was victorious. Morganton was a place where your manhood was tested. If you were unable to defend yourself then you were prime beef. I remember a time when me and two others robbed a guy for his commissary. The guy didn't bother to put up a fight and the result of that was others started robbing him. You see, in prison whenever someone tries to handle you, you have to stand ground because if you don't, you may end up on your knees and I'm not talking about begging.

Months went by and everything was pretty chill until they started letting the GD's and Crips out back. There was a fight almost every day. The GD's and Crips thought that the Five Percenters we're they enemy. But this came from immaturity and not fully understanding the gang that they represented. The GD's and Crips rolled under the number six or the six-point star and their enemies rolled under the number five and the five point star. Since the Five Percenters had a five-point star on our flag and went by the name Five Percenters, they assumed we were enemies. Again, children in over their heads. I had gotten into an altercation with a guy named "T" who was giving credit for bringing the Rolling Sixties to Morganton and possibly the state of North Carolina. We were all out on the rec yard one day and me and a guy from my city was chopping it up. He asked me about the Queen City Kings, and I told him we are descendants of Vice Lords. The n*** "T" overheard our conversation and said "Vice Lords? Man you a slob". I didn't know what slob meant but I knew it was a disrespectful word. "What the fuck you just called me nigga. I asked. "Man, you heard me, I said you a slob" I went for the dumbbell in the wight piled and was stopped by my homie from Charlotte. "Scoe chill nigga." He spoke. I looked and about a dozen Crips surrounded us. I was nervous but I couldn't let it show, so instead I said " you got this" but I didn't back down and my man pretty much sold me out. A few days later, one of the Crips decided to disrespect one of the Gods. We were all on our bunks. Some people had their tents up. Tents were really blankets that guys use to shield their bunks to have privacy while they play with themselves. I remember being stretched out reading my lessons when I heard the commotion. I put my lessons down and leaned up to see what was going down. At that moment my main man King came over to me with a scowl on his face. " What's going on" I asked. "Man's this nigga Wise letting a Crip disrespect him and he just sitting on the bunk and not saying shit" I stood up and told King let's go see what's up. "Man, I'm telling you, the God got to do something" King said as we continued to walk over. By the time we got to the other side of the dorm there was about seven or eight guys stand next to Wise bed. "What's up?" I asked once we were in earshot. At that moment the Crip

141

began spitting in Wise's face and the God remained on his top bunk. King then swung on the Crip and another Crip went to help his homie. I grab the Crip neck from behind and put him in a chokehold. King and the other Crip were fighting as I kept a tight grip on the other one. Everyone backed away as the fight went down. Seconds later the CO's ran into the dorm. I took off running and jumped back on my bunk and played sleep. I had left the guy unconscious on the floor. They snatched King and the Crip up and escorted them out. I remained on the bunk for another ten minutes before getting up and heading towards Wise. "Nigga you go do something " I said to Wise. He" nodded his head and slid out the bunk. "What y'all niggas think y'all about to do" one of the Crips asked as he too jumped off his bunk. My "A Like" needs a one on one. A Likes is the term we use as Five Percenters. It means we think Alike because we are Gods. "We don't do one on ones" he said. The began walking up and four other Crips followed. We were outnumbered but my right-hand man was gone to the hole, so it wasn't a need for me to be free. I started walking towards the TV area and the Crips followed. "Look man" I said, give the God a fair one". The Crip smirked and said " F*** that n***." At that moment I swung on him, and it went down. He slammed me hard onto the table and hopped on top of me. He was getting the best of me until Wise punched him in the face. It didn't hurt him, but it made him pause long enough for me to get from under him. He grabbed me and I headbutted him causing him to let go. I began swinging combinations to his head and chest until the CO's ran in and broke us up. As they took us out, we were headed to the Lt. Office. While being escorted, I seen them bringing King and the Crip back. "Damn I said to myself" I thought they were taken to the hole. Once in the Lt office I was seated across from a redneck hillbilly with a reddish hue. "Look" he said." I don't give a fuck if you niggers kill yourselves. If I could, I'll give all you niggers weapons and watch you kill each other like the animals you are. I'm not going to lock y'all in the hole, I'm sending you back to your dorms. Now get the fuck out of my face." I jumped up and tried launch at him but was grabbed by two CO's. The Lt. laughed. We were sent back to our dorm. Once I was back in the dorm, I knew this shit wasn't over. The next morning the officer told everyone to go outside so they can clean up the dorm. Me and King knew that the Crips we're going to retaliate. All the Gods had gone to work, and we were the only two who didn't have a job. When the officer made the announcement me and King went into the bathroom and acted like we were shitting. "Damn God it's to many of them niggas" I said. King shook his head and said, "yea it's about forty of them niggas" "Damn we in a fucked-up situation. We got to stay on this toilet God". After everyone cleared out, we were still on the toilet. About ten minutes later the officer looked into the bathroom and said " y'all need to wrap it up now and go on outside." Me and King looked at each other and said "Fuck it" at the same time. We both got up

143

and went to take our medicine like men. We stepped outside and headed towards the rec yard. " Yo God I'm going to shoot some hoops, what's up you are coming" King asked. "Nah, I'm go chill and keep my eyes on those Crips over there I said". We both looked in the direction of the Crips and it was about forty to fifty of them in a huddle. "Man Fuck them". King said and handed me a cigarette. He went to the court and started balling. I pulled on my cigarette staring at the Crips. They looked over at me occasionally as they huddled. Some even looked over at King while he was balling. I knew then that they were discussing our fate. I continued to pull on my cigarette. At that moment of about six Crips started walking towards me. I flicked to butt off my cigarette and started walking towards them. After about three steps, I thought it would be wise to put my back against the wall. So, I began to back up to the wall. The Crips rushed in and we got it in. After about five seconds which seemed like forever, I heard someone screaming out Allah-U-Akbar. It was my man King running towards me to jump in. Now it was six against two. We fought like hell, and I was doing everything I could to keep from hitting the ground. Blows was coming from the left and right of me. But I kept swinging like my life depended on it. Finally, the guards came and started making everyone. Two officers grabbed me while my eyes were burning like hell. As I was being escorted to the hole, I could see a Crip coming from commissary. Although my eyes were burning, I was still able to see. Once we were close enough,

144

I punched him in the face. The officer slammed me on the ground and yelled " help" more officers came to restrain me. I was picked up off the ground and carried to the hole.

Chapter 15

What the Fuck

Sitting in the hole I thought about my mom. She never let me down and has always been by my side. In fact, if it wasn't for my mom my bids would have been detrimental. She showed up for every court date and whenever she was allowed to catch a ride, she would come visit me. My mom wrote me every single week and never missed a week. I don't know what I would have done without her. She is indeed the best mom ever. I called collect so much that her phone bill was a thousand dollars once. She couldn't send me money that often because my dad who was getting high would smoke it up. There were times I had to rob other inmates to survive because the prison wasn't feeding us too well. It was the survival of the fittest and I was sure as hell fit for this. About two days later I was taken from the 16th floor and was put on o think was the 14th floor. If I'm not mistaken, the hospital was on the 15th floor. I remained in the hole on the 14th floor for two weeks before I was sent to the 10th floor in the building. I was put into a cell but the next day I was put into the day room. After about a week in the day room some shit was about to pop off with the Crips and of course I was on the front line. An officer whose name I don't recall grabbed me and escorted me on to the elevator. This officer was cool and also a member of the Nation of Islam. He used to build with the Gods. The Nation of Gods and Earth's (Five Percenters) had the same literature as the Nation of Islam because Clearance 13X who is the founder of the Five Percenters was a member of the N.O.I. and left to teach the children. "Man, I ain't get a chance to do nothing. Why are you grabbing me?" "Just chill out. I promise you'll thank me later. Right now, I'm saving you for something that's coming in the future" he said. I had no idea what he was speaking on. He was always straight forward. We took the elevator all the way down and then came back up. By the time we stepped onto the floor everything had calmed down. "What's up?" I asked one of the Gods. "Oh, everything straight now it was just a misunderstanding" he said. With that I got back onto my bunk. I believe the next day I was sent back to honor grade outback. "Abell!! " An officer yelled. "Yo!" "Get your shit, you are going back outside" I jumped up and got ready. I was eager to get back outside to freedom. I left the little bit off commissary I had with the Gods. Although I knew they would be ok because it was the GODS who had the kitchen on lock, and they made sure that all the Gods got a healthy portion. When in the building, the food comes to you on a cart pushed by the prisoners. Everyone would line up to receive their portion and it was the prisoners

147

who served you. If you were locked in your cell, you would take the foo back with you. I gathered my belongings and followed the officer onto the elevator, and it was the same officer who had grabbed me the day before. " Just keep cool kid" he said as we went down the elevator. He asked me to have I been studying my lessons and I replied that I have. So, he asked me the days mathematics and I told him. We finally made it outback and I was assigned to another dorm I think it was called Dog or D dorm. I was a little upset to not be going back to my previous dorm, but what the hell at least I was back. I walked into the dorm and was greeted by the Gods. My man New York was in the same dorm as me and we chopped it up for a minute.

My man New York also went by the name Wise. He was a Five Percenter too. After talking with him, my man King called me to the back of the dorm. The back was where everyone sneaked to go smoke. I must say, I never had to buy a cigarette ever again while I was there. Me and King kicked it for a while before the God Righteous pulled up on us. Lord Dignity, I just want to take my hat off to you. "I heard how you held your own even though you were outnumbered, you represented for the Gods" He handed me a pack of cigarettes and it turned into a smoke party. We all laughed about it and got ready for bed since it was already dark by the time, I made it out back. The next morning, I went to breakfast. Me and two other Gods including King decided to smoke on side of the building. This area was off limits until a certain time, so we had to be careful not to get caught. After finishing our smoke, we went back into the dorm and the guard was raising hell. He was taking his problems out on all the prisoners. I mean he was doing the most. This caused trouble. The prisoners were upset. A few guys started saying disrespectful things to the guard but was hiding while they did it. I sat on my bunk watching everything unfold. After a while I became hyped with all the excitement. While everyone else was yelling and screaming derogatory words I decided to throw a bar of soap at the officer. I missed him by inches. It wasn't long after when more guards showed up and forced everyone to go to their designated areas. Going Home. The next morning, I was laying on my bunk when the first shift officer told me I was wanted at the Lt. Office. At first, I thought someone talked about the soap being thrown but when I got in the office it was nothing like that. I was told that I was going home and that it might be Monday before I can leave. I didn't give a fuck. I was going home in about three days. I walked fast as hell back to the dorm very excited.

Once in the dorm, I told everyone the good news. Me and King sat in the day room watching videos and eating deep dish pizza from the commissary. I see the God Wise stop and speak with another God. The God pointed in my direction and Wise headed over. "Peace to the Gods" he greeted. "Peace!!" We greeted back. Wise sat down and explain to us about the situation with another God in another dorm. Apparently, the God got caught eating pork in the bathroom and the Gods held a Cipher about it. It was agreed that the God be exiled after he gave his bond that he didn't eat it. Justice was served and the God received a Universal Beat Down (UBD). I told Wise I was leaving in a couple of days, but he didn't show the same enthusiasm as the others. " Since you are leaving God, let me get your lessons so I can give them to my student." Wise asked. I agreed to give it to him since I knew them verbatim. We remained in the day room for a couple more hours watching TV. The day room was small and had two TVs on both ends. It also had two wooden tables and a microwave. Besides that, it wasn't much else. The officer yelled for chow and everyone began running out to eat. "Abell!" The officer yelled. " Yeah, what's up?" I asked, "Pack up, you are going home". "Huh, I thought I leave Monday. That's what the Lt. said." Welp you got lucky. Now get the hell on" I dapped everyone up and headed out. Back in Hidden Valley I was released from Morganton Highrise May 14th, 1996. One week after my birthday.

Chapter 16

Original Kings

I remember getting off the Greyhound in downtown Charlotte and walked a few miles to my auntie Peggy house who stayed on Summit Ave behind the Johnson C. Smith College. It took me 45 minutes to get there. Once there I called my mom to come pick me up. I've been gone for a while and was now 18 years old. When I got home it was dark and my father told me that my partner Shug wanted to see me. Shug was short and dark brown skinned. He had a hustle out this world. I've watched him sell eighteen ounces of coke in all eight balls in one day. Shug was loved all over the city. This is what helped him in his hustle. Many viewed Shug as an angry and mean guy. This was because of how he looked as well as his rough and deep voice. However, although Shug was a real hustler, he would still cut a few corners here and there. I didn't get up with Shug until the next day and we rode around Hidden Valley. He took me to go meet other Kings in the hood who had been recruited. He introduced me to some youngsters that was supposedly under my man Rolland authority. Everyone else was locked up. Ready, Boskee, Rolland, High Times, Kool Aid was dead, and the hood had change. Instead of eight or nine of us it was about a hundred. After we rode around for a while we headed back to Shug's house. He broke down how the rank structure was within the Hidden Valley Kings. There was really no structure. There was O.K.'s (Original Kings) and there was just Kings. In the beginning there was only two O.K.'s per hood.

The main hoods were Cedar Green, Hidden Valley, North Charlotte, and Dalton Village. However, Dalton Village faded away in a short period of time. While I was locked up, Hidden Valley Kings were at war with Kaos Klan Kings (North Charlotte). The war started behind a simple mistake, but that mistake was deadly. Even till this day Hidden Valley and North Charlotte relationship is strained. I was only home for a week before I was back on the block hustling. It's been five years and the hood were filled with new faces. It really wasn't new faces. It was just youngins' who had grown up. I remember walking down Wellingford Street headed to the corner store, and I saw Paco sitting on his mother's porch. The last time I had seen him he was about 9 years old. He's still pretty much looked the same except he was now taller a lot taller than me. I didn't say anything to him I mean mug him and kept walking towards the store. As I was walking back down the street Paco was still sitting on the porch, so I stopped in front of his mother's house still mean mugging him. Then I smiled and threw up the "hvk" sign and told him to walk with me. We chopped it up for about an hour or two. It wasn't long before the others from the younger generation came to my mom's house to meet me. All of them were claiming Kings. There was Paco, BZ, T, Cola, B-Man, Ty-fly, and others. After our meeting everyone went their separate ways. I called Shug for more product, and he pulled up with a guy named Baby Joc and introduced us. Baby Joc was from another hood called Barrington Oaks and was supposed to be Shug's shooter. After being home for only a week, I was back on my bullshit. I made it be known that nobody could hustle on the block unless they were Kings and I stood on that. Those who were hustling while I was gone act confused about my position on the matter. But after a few gun shots were thrown their way, they got the picture. I was only 18 and felt 30. After Shug left I headed towards the block to get my hustle on. Once I reached the block, I seen Cola leaning up against the street sign rolling a blunt. He greeted me with the King handshake and passed me the blunt. I took about three pulls and handed it back. As Cola was pulling on the blunt a black Jeep pulled up and started shooting in his direction. We both got to ducking and running for cover. The jeep speeded off. I was pissed. "Who the fuck was that" I asked Cola. " Man, I don't know homie" I looked at Cola with disbelief. "You not strapped?" I asked. "I don't have it on me because it's an SK simi-automatic and too big to walk with" "Man fuck that, go get that motherfucker now" Cola looked at me in disbelief. "What! You scared?" "Nah I'm not scared". "You know what, I'll bring that bitch here.

Let's go get it." We went to Cola house and got the gun. I walked down Springview with the assault rifle in broad daylight and put it behind some bushes on the corner of Wellingford and Springview. I then told Cola to watch his gun until I get back and if that jeep come back don't hesitate to let off. I jogged to my house and paged Shug. He called back in about 5 minutes. I told him I needed a pistol and he met me on the block 15 minutes later. He handed me a 44. Bulldog revolver. After that day, Hidden Valley would never be the same. WAR ZONE The year 1996 was a wild year. Short after I came home, I began running people out the hood who didn't belong. We were also getting into shootouts left and right. Well actually it was just me busting back at intruders who tried to move in on our turf. It was only the younger generation out there with me because everyone else was locked up.

After being home for over a month I was arrested for arm robbery. I remember getting a call about a gun. A junkie called and said he knew someone selling a gun and he told me his name. The name sounded familiar, but I wasn't sure. OK told the junkie to pick me up from my mother's house. A short while later he pulled up with another person who I didn't know. I got into the back seat, and we headed to the guy house who was selling the gun. First, I asked them to stop by my homie Keenan house who lived only about five houses down. I ran inside and told Keenan that I was about to buy a gun and when I told him who I was buying the gun from, Keenan got excited. While rubbing his hands he said" oh that's a lick. That nigga got bread. Hold up let met grab my shit, I am going with you." Keenan had become a notorious robber while I was locked up. I told Keenan that I was going alone and that we don't know what we are walking into. "Man, f*** that I'm going." Keenan said. I sighed and looked at the floor while shaking my head." This nigga!" I said to myself. When Keenan went into the next room to get his gun, I quickly exited his mom house and jumped in the car. "Go,go,go!" I said to the driver. We headed to our destination which was only several blocks in the hood.

We pulled up to the Countryside apartments inside the Hidden Valley Community. We all got out the car and headed towards the guy apartment which was located upstairs. The junkie knocked on the door and a chubby guy answered the door. We all stepped inside. I had taken about 8 valium pills earlier and was on a cloud not to mention it had me thinking I was in a dream. Once inside the apartment I immediately noticed that there was three people in the apartment already. Two women and a man. At that moment I decided to rob the house but first I need to make sure there was no one else inside. I asked to use the bathroom. The guy of the house showed me where the bathroom was. After coming out I could still hear them talking in the living room, so I began looking into the bedrooms. There was no one else here. So, I went back into the bathroom to flush the toilet so that they would hear it. I went back into the living room and asked to use the phone. I grabbed the phone off the kitchen wall and pretended to be talking to someone as I studied everyone. I was so high, unknowingly to me, I never dialed a number and the man of the house noticed this and knew something was up. I hung up the phone and asked" So, what kind of gun you got for sell". The junkie who brought me responded" he got a 380. Caliber". As I'm talking and listening, I'm also paying attention to the man of the house. I see that he was trying to get something from under the couch cushions, but he was being discreet about it. I knew right then that he was reaching for a gun. I quickly pulled my 44 bulldogs off my hip and pointed it at everyone. "Nobody move" I said and walked quickly over to the man of the house and grabbed what was under the cushion. It was a chrome 380. Now I had both guns aimed at everyone. I made everyone stand in a huddle while I took the man of the house into the bedrooms and took everything of value. I then pointed my gun at the junkie and told him let's go. We headed downstairs and I forgot that I left my shades on the coffee table. " Don't move!" I spoke. I ran back up the stairs and into the apartment. My shades were where I left them. I grabbed my shades and apologized to the people. I don't remember doing this, but it was in my motion and was probably true. They said I talked about black empowerment and how the system put guys like me in uncompromising positions to survive. I told them I was sorry and left back out. When I got to the bottom of the stairs the junkie was still there. We hopped into his car and sped off. A short while later, I was back on the block. Once I reached the block, I seen a few old homies posted up. I was telling them about what just went down and was counting the money. About 20 minutes later a car drove up and started shooting at us or me. I quickly began returning fire with both pistols. I don't think I hit anyone, but I do remember their back and side window being shattered. Everyone took off running through the path. The path would take us from Wellingford to Cinderella Rd. We had to jump the creek. Once we reached Cinderella Rd., we began jogging towards Munsee St. As we started walking up Munsee Rd., we seen two brothers that we were all cool with. They sold weed in the hood and back in those days they kept that fire. Big D was with me and wanted to be some wood. We approached the two brothers and one of them asked if I was the one shooting over in Beechway. I told him no as I watched Big D get his shit from the other brother. "Man, why would you ask some shit like that?" My Lil homie Ty asked. "Nah, I was just asking because I know Scoe be doing the most shooting down there. That's all". After Big D got the weed, we headed towards the hotel room on Sugar Creek. A chick I was fucking was at the room with Big D baby mom waiting on us. As we continued walking, we heard the brothers say be careful. We had just reached Yuma St. and a police car was riding slowly towards us. I was wearing a big ass afro wig and was trying to adjust it on my head. I don't

157

remember where I got it from, but it had to be right before the shootout. The police kept coming towards u at a slow pace. "Don't nobody run" I said. Once the cops got beside us, I seen three doors open up and three cops jumped out. I immediately took off running because I had two guns on me. I ran down Yuma St. and through someone yard. A helicopter was above me. I have no idea where it came from and how it got there so fast. I continued running and jumping fences. I had to get those guns off of me quick. I slung the guns in opposite directions and kept it moving. Somehow the helicopter was hovering right above me shining it's light. Although it was now night the copters light made it appear as if it was daylight. I was caught and slammed to the ground. Two officers carried me to the police car and placed me in the back seat. " What the fuck y'all chasing me for" I asked. The officer turned to look at me and replied" nothing yet, just sit tight for now" I remained silent thinking to myself what the hell was this about. Not long after one of the officers found the 380. And another officer found my 44. They both brought the guns over to the officer whose car I was sitting in. The officer stepped out and spoke to the others. There were about six or seven police cars parked every which way. After a moment another police car pulled up with about three people in it. They all got out and approached me in the backseat. They were identifying me to the cops. It was the people I robbed. The officer got back in the patrol car. "What am I being charged with?" I asked again. The officer turned around with a smile and said, " you're being charged with arm robbery and possession of firearms" " I didn't rob nobody and y'all didn't get no guns off me." I spoke. The officer drove away as we headed downtown to the jail. I was booked and charged with arm robbery and possession of a firearm. I called my mother to let her know I was in the county. I knew she couldn't post the bond I was given so I didn't even ask.

Chapter 17

Federal Inmates

After my call I was dressed out and sent to my pod. A couple of days later I was sent to Spector Drive. Specter Drive was another part of Charlotte jail on the other side of town. These were trailers that had a fence around it. I was escorted to my trailer and assigned a bunk. There was a lot of federal inmates waiting to be sentence. This was 1996 and the jail was full of federal inmates. There was an old coon who slept above me and had one side of the pod on lock.

Couldn't nobody use the phone before him, and he used it all day. One day I had to use the phone and went to grab it. About two or three guys approached me and said that the phone belongs to the older guy. This was my first time having to do time around adults. I had been doing juvenile bids and had a child's mentality. So, I immediately became hostile and aggressive." I don't give a fuck who y'all think this phone belongs to. I need to get out, I have a bond to make" I said to one of the guys. The pod got extremely quiet as everyone waited to see what would happen. The shorter guy looked at me and said," I don't know who you think you is..." " Roscoe. My name's Roscoe. That's who I am" I said. I gripped the phone handle tightly so I could use it as a weapon. Before it got out of hand the old man stood up and told the guys to fall back and let me use the phone. "You're lucky pops said to let you use the phone". The shorter guy spoke again. " Man, I was going to use this motherfucker anyway" I said as I began dialing my mom's number. After speaking with my mother and letting her know my court date I decided to go outside. There was recreational equipment. There might have been a basketball goal but I'm not sure. Everyone was fenced in, but we were able to communicate with other prisoners in other trailers. Many was older than I and most was federal inmates. I met a kid who was from the neighborhood Greer town and said he was a five Percenter. We began building by going over the lessons. After that day, we would build every day. After I went back inside, I jumped in the shower checked my account. My mom had sent money so the next day I went to commissary. Back then we used to walk to the commissary. On this particular day I ran into a childhood friend who was in another dorm. We chopped it up and he told me he was in for bank robbery. He was on his way to the feds I got back to my bunk and went through my commissary. The old head who controlled the phone approached me. "What up young blood?". I stood up, "shiiid what's up?". I said with my face balled up. "I just wanted to make sure everything was good with us" " I'm good. I just need to use that phone". "You can use the phone young blood". He reached out his hand and I shook it. I went to court the following week and my bond wasn't lowered. As soon as I got back in the dorm, I started making phone calls to post bond. Everyone was locked up except Shug and Keenan so those were the two I looked towards to getting me out. It took me about a week after my court date to make bond. My dad and neighbor picked me up and we headed towards the house. On the drive home my dad told me that Keenan said for me to stay in the house until he came through to speak with me. Once home I called Keenan to let him know I was out. 30 minutes later he pulled up in a white Acura sport coupe. Keenan was a light skinned cat that spoke with a slur. He laughed at everything. He loved cracking jokes. But don't let the joking fool you. Keenan was as deadly as a rattlesnake. His hustle was robbing dope boys. Keenan stayed plotting. This also caused him to be in many dangerous altercations. But Keenan was death struck and accepted all that came with it. He also had a good heart towards the people he loved. If he could help you in any kind of way, he would do it. I stepped outside and we kicked it. He told me that he gave my mom five bands to get me out. I told him I appreciate what he did and that I would pay him back for it. He then pulled out an egg of dope which was 28 grams. "Look, I charge nine hundred dollars for each egg. But I need you to give me back twelve hundred. " Keenan told me. "That's cool" I said. An egg was almost going for that price anyway. He then told me to ride with him to his mother's house. Once in the house he went into the closet and pulled out a bag. He laid the bag on the bed and pulled out a big ass bag of dope. "You see this here; this is a kilo and it's yours" I looked at the dope and smiled. I started calculating all the money I could make. I reached for the dope and he stopped me. "What's up?" I asked. "Man, I'm not giving you all this shit at one time I already know where that's going to lead us. It's yours because I'm not going to sell it to no one. Every time you re-up I'm going to grab your dope from this bag. I'm charging you 1200 an ounce. The extra 300 goes towards what you owe me. Each time you sell an ounce, it takes off 300." I began calculating again. That means I would have to sell at least 16 ounces to pay this nigga back. I was a little hesitant at first but said Fuck it because in those days I would make thee thousand off the egg, so we did the King handshake as an agreement. Later that night, me Keenan and Black Travis who was another friend of ours went to the club named The Arena. We didn't go inside, we just chilled in the parking lot. It was more people in the parking lot than inside the club. " Boy it's packed tonight" said Keenan as he handed me the blunt. "Hell yeah" Black Travis responded. " Hella bitches too" There was girls everywhere dancing to music from cars that was driven by the hustlers. As we smoked the weed and watch the scene a girl approached Keenan. "What's up Keenan" the girl asked after Keenan rolled down his window. "Ain't shit, what you are doing out here looking all good and shit" Keenan asked, "I'm chilling, I just came to speak and see how you were doing" "You can tell by the whip I'm driving that I'm doing good" " Yea I can see, but I didn't come over here for that. I just want to give you the heads up that some guy you supposedly robbed is out here somewhere" " What nigga? Keenan asked. "I don't know him, but I heard one of them say that you were in the parking lot and told the others to be safe." "Oh yeah, well fuck them niggas. Where they at right now?". I don't know, I think they all left but I just wanted to give you the heads up because you my nigga" " I appreciate it" Keenan said and he turned towards me. " You heard what that bitch said" I handed Keenan the blunt and blew the smoke out my nose. " Yeah, I heard her. Fuck them niggas" I said lifting my pistol up to show Keenan what I mean. Keenan looked at Black Travis and asked, "are you good?". "I'm not strapped ". Black Travis complained. Keenan inhaled the weed smoke and said, " don't trip me and Scoe got this" I turned to Black and said " yeah, everybody knows when it comes to serving beef, I'm the best chef in the city because I'm going to serve them hard and done". We all began laughing as Keenan pulled off. We cruised the parking lot for a while until we rode up on Keenan's older brother and his friends. After a couple of minutes if just shooting the shit, a grey Range Rover pulled up. We were still seated in the car. I was high as hell. I had taken about 6 or 7 Valiums earlier and was tap-dancing on the sun. The guys in the Range began talking to Keenan's brother. After a couple of minutes, the volume of their conversation went up and I could tell that the guys in the jeep were Jamaicans. They began arguing back and forth. They did this for another minute before Keenan jumped out with his pistol in hand. He told the Jamaican to pull off. The guy seen the gun and slowly pulled off with his hands up. Keenan then jumped back in the car. We continued to smoke weed and talking to his brother until someone yelled out "they are coming back around Keenan!". "Who coming back around I asked?". At that moment we heard gun shots. I sucked down in the seat trying to listen where the shot was coming from. Keenan jumped out the Acura Coupe and return fire. The jeep speeded off. Keenan jumped back in the car and gave chase. As we got closer to the fleeing jeep, I leaned out the passenger window and let off 5 or 6 shots at the jeep. Keenan was dumping out the driver window. The Jamaicans lost control of the jeep and hit a telephone pole. A cop car was parked near a gas station and seen what happened. "Oh shit, there go the police" Black Travis yelled out. The cop began to chase us as Keenan accelerated. We were flying down a dark street. I can't remember the name of the street. Keenan turned off the headlights and punched it. I was holding on for dear life because I couldn't see shit. I yelled out to Keenan asking him what the fuck was he doing. " Man chill I got this shit" Keenan said as he was doing his thing with the car. " Nigga how the fuck you got something when we can't see shit" I asked. " The police can't see shit neither". Keenan replied. I looked back at the cop car that was a couple hundred feet behind us and said" that motherfucker got his lights on, he can see" " yea but he can't see us" Keenan said. And he was right, we got away. BACK ON THE BLOCK A couple days later I was on the block. I had just bust down a whole egg and headed to block. I believe I cut up a little over three thousand worth. I took about five hundred worth and left the rest at my mom's house. We were posted on the block about eight deeps. As me and Paco was slap boxing, Boskee pulled up in a rental car. " What's up King he yelled out the window. I reached for my pistol. Hold, hold, hold I heard Boskee say. I looked and recognized him. I smiled and walked up to the car. "What up King" I said approaching the car." What's up with you Joe? " Bo said stepping out the car. We have each other love by doing the King handshake." I see you done got out" I said. Me and Bo chopped it up until he had to go see his probation officer. " Aye, I'm coming back later on, so we can kick it" Bo said. I'll be here I said as Bo pulled off. I began walking towards Cesar's Ford apartments when Paco asked where I was going." I'm going to get a cigar to smoke this weed I got from Keenan" I said. " Hold up I'm walking with you". Paco jogged to catch up. We walk through the apartments and through the path that leads to the store. Once at the store I grabbed two cigars and headed back out. Once outside I seen Paco talking to an older Partner of mine.

He weighed about five hundred pounds and his car had no seats because it couldn't support his weight. We stood outside his car smoking weed and talking. After about a minute or so, he asked us to jump in. We began riding throughout the hood. Paco, who was high as hell kept giggling. "What's so damn funny" I whispered to him already knowing. Paco whispered back saying " man that nigga fat as hell" We both bust out laughing. We continued to ride around smoking weed. Finally, I asked that we be dropped off on Snow White. After he drove off me and Pac stood on the corner of Snow White and Spring Garden smoking. Let's go stand by the bus stop in case the police pull up. It wasn't five minutes before the police came fucking with us. Paco through the blunt on the ground and I swallowed the little bit I had left. The cop called for backup, and it was at this point where all hell broke loose. The second cop claimed to have found some dope on the ground by the bus stop. "Oh, hell naw, where you get that shit from?" I said in disbelief. "I saw you throw it when I pulled up" the cop responded. "Man, I ain't had no dope on me" I did have dope on me, but they didn't find it when I was searched. I kept the dope between my butt cheeks. It was at that moment I knew they were setting us up and I had already made my mind up. The cop grabbed my arm and proceeded to cuff me. I quickly broke loose and took off running. The police gave chase. I ran down Snow White and jumped a fence into someone back yard. I ran through the front yard and onto Bilmark avenue. I never looked back to see where the police were, I just kept running until I made it to my mother's house. I was worried that the cops would show up there, so I walked down to Beechway apartments. Once I reached the apartments BZ came out the cut and asked where Paco go. "Man, I left him on

Snow White. The police were chasing me" I said. "Damn did Pac get away?". " They weren't chasing him. One of the cops lied and said he seen me throw some dope down. You know I wasn't going for that, I bailed on they ass." BZ started laughing. About fifteen minutes later Paco came walking down Springview. Once he reached us, he said, " boy you took off like the road runner" and we all laughed. Later that night Boskee came to my mother's house, and we drove up to Hershey apartments. It was there that I noticed that my valium pills were missing and that someone had taken them. I exploded. "Man, somebody stole my pills" I said to Bo. "When was the last time you seen them" he asked. "Shiid, in Beechway" I said. We jumped into Bo's Cadillac and headed to Beechway. There was about ten to twelve people standing out there when we pulled up. I hopped out with my pistol in hand. "What you finna do, rob them? Bo asked. I didn't respond. I walked up the hill screaming " who got my shit?" Everyone looked confused. No one owned up to it, so out of frustration, I held everyone at gun point. Paco and BZ ran over "What's up Scoe"? They asked while Paco held a 38 revolver. "One of these niggas got my pills" I said. Paco pointed his weapon at the crowd and said, " where my nigga shit?", Everyone began ducking. "Scoe, I got yo shit." BZ said. "How you get my shit?" "You gave it to me earlier because you said Every time you take to many you go to jail. So, you left them with me.". I was so shell of them pills that I forgot all about it. "Where they ate, I asked?". BZ handed me the pills. Bo got out the car and walked over. "Y'all niggas crazy". He said while shaking his head. "Fuck that!". I spoke. Me, Bo, Paco and BZ jumped in the Cadillac and began smoking.

While we smoked, Bo was giving the youngins' game. Paco was one of those people who was like a sponge. He soaked everything up. He was pretty much mature for his age. I remember on two different occasions where he saved my life. The first time was when I was on the run and the bounty hunter jumped out on me. I had my back turned and didn't see him. Paco yelled out my name. I turned just in time to see the bounty hunter running towards me. I took off running and for the first time and only time I looked back to see where he was because he had such a head start. As I looked over my shoulder, I seen Paco running right behind him and he clipped his legs causer the bounty hunter to fall. The rest was history. I got away again.

Chapter 18

My Baby Mama

WAR 1996 some guys from New York moved into Beechway apartments. We weren't tripping on people moving into our hood. But we did trip if you thought you were going to get money. On one occasion I had to let them know that they couldn't sell dope in our hood. I thought we had an understanding until they shot Black Travis. Black Travis told us the story when we went to see him in CMC (Carolina Medical Center) Hospital. Apparently, one of the New York guys was still trying to hustle after we had that conversation. Black Travis had gotten into a heated argument him. The guy went into the apartment as Black Travis was getting into a car. As Black was about to pull off, the guy came out the apartment with two more guys and they began shooting up the car that Black was in. He was hit by an assault rifle. I even think that the news had pronounced him dead, but he came back. When me, Shug, Keenan, and Keenan's baby mom left the hospital, I told Shug we got to get these niggas. That night me, Shug, and a couple more guys headed to the New York niggas apartment. Shug and another homie crept to the back door just in case whoever inside tried to escape. Me and my man Cola went to the front door. I told Paco to watch the parking lot. I counted to three, letting Cola get ready. On the third count I kicked in the front door, and we rushed inside. I was holding my gun up coming in. It was dark inside, and I thought I seen someone, so I shot about three times. After the first shot, I heard Cola yell out "oh shit". I squeezed two more times. Everything was quite for a split second and then the back door came crashing in. I almost shot Shug as he came through the back door. Once inside Shug whispered my name. At that moment, the streetlights peered into the apartment from the front door, and I was able to see. Paco ran to the front door " what the fuck was that" he asked coming in through the front. " You supposed to be watching the front door" I told him. " Fuck that, I heard shots". We all began to search the place. There was nothing inside. Mad and frustrated, we left. The next morning, I was standing on the block when Shug pulled up in his white drop top BMW. " What's up, ain't nobody seen them niggas yet?" He asked. I told him not yet. We drove up to my mom's house and parked his car and we both walked down to Beechway. After about 30 minutes we decided to walk to the African store for a blunt. As we began to walk, I pulled out a bag of powder and started snoring it up my nose as we walked down the street. Shug started laughing at me saying I'm crazy. I ignored him and kept snorting. We had almost reached the store when Shug yelled out "look!" And pointed towards the Hidden

Valley barber shop I looked in that direction. "You see that?" He asked. There was three men jogging through the path behind the shop that leads into Beechway apartments. "Hell, yeah I see them" I responded. Just like in a movie, Keenan swerved up in his Suburban at the same time we were watch the niggas jog. Keenan yells out the driver window "one of them niggas who shot Black just went into Wendy's with a bitch"." Yea and we just seen three of them running through the cut" I told him.

At that moment, we knew what to do. Me and Shug went after the jogging niggas as Keenan accelerated towards Wendy's. Once we got to Beechway we seen a green Cherokee just pulling in. Once they seen me and Shug running up the New York niggas began ducking behind the jeep. I immediately began shooting in their direction. Shug stretch out on the pavement and began shooting upwards as he laid on his stomach. I aimed at the jeeps driver window because I had seen someone behind the wheel. I fired about four shots from my new .44 bulldog. It was over in a matter of seconds. The New York niggas retreated as we gave chase. I ran to the back of the apartments that led to the path. I see four guys running towards the barbershop. One of them had been hit as he was holding his arm while running. As I continued to chase so I can finish my job, three police cars pulled into the shops parking lot. I immediately duck and turned around. Me and Shug ran to my mom's house. I was tired as hell from all that running, and my heart was racing. I had snorted about two grams of coke. We jumped in the BMW and headed to Barrington Oaks to lay low. Shug paged Keenan and he met us in the Oaks. Keenan was able to get the nigga that he seen in Wendy's, but he caught him in Delahey Courts. He said when he was pulling into Wendy's, they were pulling out, so he got behind them and caught them at the store in Delahey. After we left Barrington Oaks, we headed towards Tangle Woods. Keenan said he had something to do so he went another way. Once in Tangle Wood we stopped by my man Hype crib. We chopped it up for a few. Hype was a laid-back brother. He had a pimp like swag. I met Hype around 1991 at Street Academy when we were in the 7th grade. I hadn't seen him for a while until I ran into him at the High Rise. After about an hour, me and Shug headed towards his house. While chilling at Shug's house, his plug pulled up. I stepped outside with Shug as he spoke with the plug. There was another guy with the plug. I studied both guys with intense concentration. I immediately knew that both guys were either Cuban or Dominican. They didn't appear to be a threat, so I relaxed a little, but only a little. After Shug took care of his business, we stepped back into the house. Once in the house, Shug told me the names of the two Dominicans that were from New York. Later, I would meet the plug younger sister through a girl I was dating. This girl I will call Lay. Lay was light skinned and thick. She was also Dominican and from New York. I didn't know that Lay was the plug sister, but I did know that Lay and her sisters supplied the Beatties Ford area. Me and Lay use to say we were brother and sister because we favored. For a while I didn't know that Lay was Dominican. It wasn't until we were at a room on Sugar Creek that I learned. The hotel maids came into the room two deep. Both maids began speaking in English and Lay said something to them in Spanish. The spoke in this language for about five minutes before I asked Lay where she learned Spanish." Roscoe, I'm Dominican" she said. I looked at her in disbelief. After all this time I never knew. I dated Lay best friend who was a single mother. I was eighteen and she was twenty-eight. The girl I was dating use to sell weight with Lay until one day she got set up in McDonald's on the Ford. She went to serve a guy an ounce of coke at Mickey D's when the police swarmed in. Since she had kids, Lay took the charge for her and served a couple of years for trafficking. While still at Shug's house, his younger cousin Damien Truesdale who everyone called Kwon came over. He told me about a guy he had been plotting on for a week and was about to rob him. He asked if I was interested and of course I was down but once we went to do the lick, Kwon realized that the target was the older brother of one of his partners, so we are dead it. Kwon would eventually be murdered almost a year later. The tragic death of Damien will forever be in my mind. It seemed that he was crashing out left and right. Almost like he knew death was coming. I remember walking from the store with my girlfriend and Keenan pulled up on me. He told me he had a lick for me. Against my girl wishes, I jumped in the car. This day, Keenan was driving his mom's car. We headed to the spot to rob whoever this nigga was. Keenan told me the lick was at Davis Lake Apartments which is located on the Northwest side

of Charlotte. As we were driving up North Tryon, I seen a couple of police cars and an ambulance at the corner store on the corner of Wellingford and North Tryon Street. As we rode past, I said to myself out loud " I wonder what happened over there? They got the yellow tape up and everything." Keenan burst out laughing. I learned later that the guy apartment we were going too was the victim at the store. Apparently, Keenan, Kwon and another of my homies had tried to

kidnap the dude while he was using the payphone. Keenan told them to snatch the nigga up and take him back the crib to rob him. The guy refused to cooperate, so Kwon shot him several times. Somehow the guy lived. They did this 10 minutes before coming to get me. We finally made it to the apartment. Keenan told me that the guy girl might be in the apartment and to knock on the door. "Why don't we just kick the door in nigga" as asked Keenan. " "Man, it's better this way, trust me." Keenan said. I went and knocked on the door, but no one answered. I made my way to the back of the apartment and looked through the kitchen blinds. Keenan came up behind me. " Damn! Somebody must have told her we were coming, and she dipped." Keenan said out loud. I looked at Keenan in disbelief and said " n***** if she left then that means she took everything with her" "Man fuck that. Something in this bitch, trust me. "Nigga I don't think shit in there" I whispered. Keenan began looking around, making sure no one was watching." Shit let's find out". We bust the kitchen window out and I reached inside to unlock the window. Keenan lifted the window up and looked at me." What?" I asked. " You got to be the one to climb in. I'm too big". I looked inside the kitchen window and noticed that the entire apartment was dark. "Man, it's dark as hell in there" I said to Keenan. He looked at me and said," it's a hundred thousand dollars in there." Without thinking I was climbing through the window. I landed headfirst. I jumped up and quickly looked around the kitchen for any movement. I really couldn't see shit and was a little nervous. I kept my gun aimed at the entrance to the kitchen. I waited for my eyes to adjust to the darkness. Keenan began tapping on the back slide door. I slowly turned towards him and seen him motioning for me to open the slide door. My eyes hadn't quite adjusted to the dark yet, but I went to open the door. I unlatched the door and tried to slide it open, but it wouldn't budge. I hit the latch again and pulled on the slider, but it still wouldn't open. I almost panicked. I kept looking over my shoulder making sure no one crept up. Keenan tapped the slide door again. I looked at him and he pointed down at the stick that was in place to keep the door from opening up. I immediately snatched the stick out and let Keenan in. We began searching the place for the money. During our search, Keenan received a call on his Mobil phone. I could tell he was talking to the homie T. T and Keenan were robbing partners.

Which was strange that he wasn't here with us. As Keenan spoke with T. I continued to search the place. Keenan began yelling out to me to go and search certain areas. Keenan put up his phone and started back his search. I found nothing in the areas Keenan asked me to search. After explaining this to him, he told me that T. had called him and told him what areas to search. So, T. was in on it after all. We never found the money.

About a week later we were at it again. But this time we had two more niggas with us, and the occupants were in the house. A day or so went by and I was chilling with my partners Bo and Shug. We had gone to our favorite spot called the Gold Room which was located on Graham Street in downtown Charlotte. The Gold Room was a bar where all the older powder heads hung out. You could buy any drug in existence at that time. I see my man Big Zeek from North Charlotte and waved him over to me. He was telling me how he got robbed and shot in the leg. I explained to him that if he found out who it was to let me know and I'll handle it. We shook hands and I headed to the bar for free drinks. The bartender who was an older lady liked me a lot and would give me free drinks. I loved the Gold Room because my man from New York who was the D.J. would shout out our names

177

when we came through the door. We hung in the Gold Room for about two hours and left. We were headed back to the Valley and stopped at the Racetrack on Sugar Creek for cigars. As I was coming out the store, I seen Boskee and Shug talking to Keenan and T. I walked over and gave Keenan the King handshake and nodded at T. We talked for about five minutes before we all decided to leave. I jumped in the car with Keenan and T, and we turned into the hood. I told Bo and Shug that I'll catch back up with them later. Keenan pager started going off and he said it was Kwon. I told them to drop me off in Beechway on the way to get Kwon. After I was dropped off, I noticed that no one was on the block. There were a few junkies walking back and forth and I made a quick sixty dollars. After about an hour I was getting bored and started playing Russian roulette by myself to past time. After about ten minutes of that I was overwhelmed with boredom. I stood up and walked towards Season Ford apartments. As I stood pissing on side of the building a junkie walked up with 15 dollars. "Scoe give me a dub". I grabbed the money and pulled out my sack. I was looking down into my bag to serve her when I see bright headlights. I looked up but couldn't see what type of car it was due to the lights. "Oh shit!" The junkie yelled out." That's them New York niggas that y'all beefing with" The junkie to off running in the opposite direction. I quickly snatched my pistol off my waist and let off two rounds towards the lights. I ran behind the dumpster for cover. They never returned fire and it dawn on me that they didn't know my location. I peeked around the dumpster, and they looked to be four cars deep. I got nervous. I couldn't come out of hiding because I'll blow my location. The cars started circling around the parking lot looking for me. "Damn where everyone at" I remembered thinking to myself. I was out alone and Shug and Boskee hadn't pulled up yet. I was outnumbered so I did the only logical thing to do, I climbed inside the dumpster. The cars continued to circle. I remained still and quiet praying I didn't get caught in the dumpster knowing it would be the end of me. As I waited in the dumpster, I heard one of the niggas ask someone if they see me. " I don't see shit" came the reply. "I didn't even see where the shots came from." As I waited in the dumpster, I thought to myself " I can't sit around waiting to die so I slowly began to creep out the dumpster. As I came out headfirst, I heard gun shots. This caused me to panic as I was climbing out. At that moment it sounded as if a hundred people started shooting. My heart began racing and my mouth became dry. As I peeked around the dumpster, I seen a couple cars speeding off. One car remained still. I heard more shots. These shots sounded like multiple guns. Heart racing, I ran from behind the dumpster and began shooting at the car as it skidded off. I took off running towards Cinderella Rd. The next day I went to Wendy's and seen a friend working inside. I paid for my order and sat down. My friend walked over to me. She had her hair pulled back in a ponytail and her red lipstick complemented her dark

179

complexion." You heard what happened to Kwon last night? She asked. "Naw I paged him this morning, but he never called back" I said." He didn't call back because he's dead" I quickly looked up her. "What the fuck you mean dead?". She told me that she was walking home from work and witnessed the entire thing. When she told me the people who were involved shocked the hell out of me. " Ain't no way they did that. I was just with them niggas last night," I spoke. "Well, they did it, I saw everything". She explained how more than one person were in on it. As I listened, I knew it was a set up. I got up from the table and threw my food away. I left Wendy's and headed towards the block. As I walked, I could see from a distance that the block was full of people. "What's up" I said to everyone while giving them the King handshake. I walked over to Matty who was rolling a blunt. "I heard what happened the other night." I said to Matty. Matty looked at me as he lit up the blunt. He looked up at the sky and blew smoke out his mouth. "Man, fuck Keenan" he said. I grabbed the blunt and inhaled. "Man, y'all tripping. Y'all need to squash that," I knew it couldn't be rectified because Matty stole Five grand from Keenan about a week ago. And Keenan had been trying to catch Matty ever since. Keenan almost caught him a couple time, but Matty got away. Just the other night my pops was telling me how Matty came by the house and asked to use my baby sister Rosie bike to ride down to the block. My dad told him he could and Matty headed towards Beechway. After about one minute my dad said he seen Matty racing back to the house full speed on my sister's bike. Matty pulled up in the yard and jumped off the bike while it was still rolling and ran into the backyard. At first my pops thought the police was chasing him. A few seconds later my dad heard a car speeding. It was Keenan in his Suburban giving chase. Keenan pulled up and hopped out with his gun in hand. "Which way did he go" Keenan asked my dad. " Man, you know I can't choose sides" my father replied. As Keenan was speaking to my father, Matty shot at Keenan from behind the house. Keenan got low and started slowly creeping towards the back of the house. It was dark so Keenan couldn't see. " Stop hiding and come out nigga" Keenan screamed. Matty fired again. Keenan still couldn't pinpoint his location. "Where you at?" Keenan yelled out again. "Step on a branch or something nigga so I can find your scary ass." Boom!

Boom! Boom! Matty shot again. At this moment, Keenan had to retreat. He ran and jumped into his Suburban and speeded off. Me and Matty continued to smoke the blunt. I watched as everyone was doing their thing hustling. Wellingford was very competitive when it came grinding. In those days, it wasn't about cliental. A junkie would pull up with about ten people rushing to the car trying to get their products off. As I watched the scene before me Paco said he was walking to the BP store on Cinderella. I decided to walk with him because a few days prior I got into a shootout with some guys from

The Hidden Valley Kings

the Greenville hood located of Statesville Ave.

This was behind lil TT getting jumped at the store. After he got jumped, he staggered through the path and told us what happened. We all ran through the path and the niggas was still there. One of the seen us and alerted the others. One of them had a gun and started shooting. I returned fire and missed. Later that night we did a drive by in their hood. I walked with Pac in case they were patrolling the store looking for one of us. I told Matty I'd be right back. Me and Pac headed

to the store while smoking on the blunt I walked away with from Matty. As we walked through the path, we heard gun shots. I turned around and started running back towards the block. Pac was behind me. We reached the block only to see Matty laying on the ground with a bullet wound to the shoulder and I think the leg. Matty kept grunting that his body was on fire." What the hell happened?". I asked. I was told that Keenan pulled up to the block, shot Matty and pulled off. Gia had gone to call an ambulance. As everyone waited for the ambulance, Ready pulled up in his black 78 Fleetwood. "Get in!" He yelled to me. I jumped in the car, and we pulled off. We rode down Wellingford and turned-on North Tryon St. Once we reached Sugar Creek, Ready started venting on how Kings can't be killing Kings.

Chapter 19

Tears Weren't There

When the Kings first started out, there wasn't many. At least not in Hidden Valley. In the beginning, there was no leaders to H.V.K. because all the originals grew up together and it's hard trying to make a friend subordinate to you. We would always have a vote on any and every decision and the majority wins. It wasn't until about 94 or 95 when other Kings became subordinate to us. This was either because they were young, just joining, or wasn't a part of our immediate circle. Me on the other hand was the enforcer. It's been like that even before the Kings started. Ready continued to vent "niggas getting out of control and we need to find a way to get this shit organized." I agreed with Ready. "Who go do the organizing?" I asked. "I'm going to show you something when we get to the crib" Ready said. 10 minutes later we pulled up to Ready apartment in Tanglewood apartments. We went inside. I sat on the couch while Ready went into the back room. He returned with some paperwork. He tossed the papers on lap. "Read that!" He spoke. I looked at the papers and started reading. It was documentation on the King organization. I

183

read the paperwork and liked the contents. "Rolland wrote that while in the feds" Ready told me. " No one else has seen this paperwork but you, me and Rolland" he said. I continued to look over the paperwork. It mentioned the rank structure. There was the Supreme O.K., The Prince, The Elders, The Supreme Knights, etc. I looked up at Ready and said, " I think this might work." "Yea that's what my brother says too." Ready replied. Ready's brother Rolland was in the feds after he and some other homies was involved in a home invasion that ended up with a bunch of people getting shot. It was a set up from the beginning. After Ready and I finished going over the paperwork we rode around collecting the money owed to him. Later that night we pulled up to the Oaks apartments complex. We pull into the parking lot. I stepped out and started scanning the area looking for Shug. A youngin' walked up to me. "Y'all looking for Shug?" he asked. " Yea where that nigga at" I said. At the moment, another youngin' walked over and started explaining what happened. The youngin' told us that Shug was playing tunk for 150 a hand and Keenan pulled up. Say Keenan approached Shug lol homie Baby Jock. Jock knowing how close we all were running over to Keenan excited to show off the new gun that Shug had gave him. Jock didn't know that Shug owed Keenan for the 9 ounces he fronted him. Keenan asked to see the gun and Jock handed it over to him. Keenan then walked over to Shug and pointed the gun at him. "N*** you out here gambling with my money" Keenan screamed.

184

Keenan robbed Shug for everything in his pockets and made him come out his shoes. Shug was hurt as the tears came out his eyes. The tears weren't out of fear but of being hurt. They said Keenan had tears coming out his eyes as well as he said, " nigga you know I don't want to do this shit, but you forced my hand". After Keenan left, Shug screamed on Baby Joc for giving Keenan the pistol. We left the Oaks and headed back to the hood. Ready dropped me off and kept pushing. The next day we all went to see Matty at the hospital. He looked at me and said " that nigga got to die asap" get some rest I told him. Later I was told that a meeting was called, and that Keenan was sentenced to death. I wasn't at this meeting but for some strange reason it was said that I was chosen for the mission because I'm skilled enough to get away with it. When I found out about it, it was almost too late. We were standing outside at the Tryon Mall movies. Keenan pulled up and hopped out the car. "What's up my nigga " I said as Keenan approached only me. " I thought we were better than this. Out of all these niggas you got the biggest heart and most loyalty." I was thinking to myself "what's wrong with this nigga" that's when I noticed that Keenan had his hand placed on his gun at the hip. I didn't know what was going on, but I slowly begin reaching for my gun. Keenan sucking his teeth looked at me and said, " n*** how you go volunteer my death? "Yo what!!" I said in shock." I heard y'all had a meeting and you the one was chosen for the job". I explained to Keenan I had no idea about a meeting and that he knows me. If it was like that, I would've started shooting the moment I seen you pull into the parking lot. "You might be right, but you know I was coming." Keenan said. I looked my childhood friend in the eyes. "Like I said, we wouldn't be having this conversation." We talked a little while longer and shook hands then Keenan left. I looked at Boskee. What the fuck was he talking about a meeting. Bo told me they had a meeting about Keenan and how he was getting out of control. Also, that my name came up as being the one to do it. This pissed me off. Once I got to the house, I immediately paged Ready about the situation. He called me back and we had a heated argument. I wasn't feeling it, but I understood. Keenan was a monster in the streets and a reputation for being quick on the draw. In everyone else opinion I was one of the fewest who could match his energy. But this was my life since childhood. I was always thrown into someone else's altercations without my knowledge. I never really had personal beef. Most of my beefs came from protecting those I considered close to me. However, over the years people would do things and use my name in hopes that there would be no repercussions. This caused me to have enemies I knew nothing about. Things started getting a lil tricky in 96'. Everyone was falling out with each other. One day, High Time and Boskee pulled up to my mother house. High Times told me that ready had violated him. Violation is when you do something against KING law, and you're punished for it. Apparently, High Times and Shug's cousin

186

got into an argument at the hotel. High Times jumped on him and roughed him up pretty badly. Ready, who was in the room didn't approve of High Times bullying. So Ready violated h for putting his hands on another KING. Then he violated Shug's cousin for not fighting back. After High Times finished explaining to me, I told him not to trip. "Do you know how many times my name came up for violation." I said to High Times. " Yea but you always buck the violation so that don't count" Boskee said while turning up a bottle of 1800. "'Scoe hardheaded than a m*****" High Times said as he laughed. Like I predicted, for whatever reason, the violation never stuck. After a couple of weeks, me and Boskee was hanging out at McDonald's Inn. McDonald's Inn was a Hotel slash Bar as well as a swimming pool. We headed up stairs to the room our people had. We chilled in the room for a while before we left. We got on the elevator and headed down to the lobby. Once in the lobby I seen that the place was packed. I headed towards the bathroom and on my way, I ran into Shug and Keenan. I thought it seemed weird to see these two together after considering what happened.

Nevertheless, here they were. I spoke to them briefly before going into the bathroom. As I was taking a piss something came over me. For some reason I was feeling a little uncomfortable. After pissing I looked into the mirror and splashed water on my face. I stepped out the bathroom and immediately began scanning the area. I didn't see

187

a threat but that feeling was in the pit of my stomach. I walked over to Boskee and asked was he ready to go. He said yea and we headed for the entrance. Once outside my senses was at an all-time high. I walked while gripping the handle on my pistol. "Yo Scoe, where y'all headed to" Shug ask. I don't know yet, I'm just riding with Bo. Wherever he goes I'm going" I replied. Bo was already in the car as I began walking in that direction. I was about fifteen feet away from the passenger side when I heard the first shot. I dropped low to the ground trying to see where the shots were coming from. "Boom! Boom! Boom!" More shots ranged out. At this time, I could see sparks flying from the concrete around me. I continued to scan the parking lot. "Bingo!" I spotted my target. He was behind a black Range Rover. I started shooting in that direction. Everyone was screaming and running for cover. We continued to shoot back and forth. I used Bo Cadillac as a shield. Bo kept screaming for me to get in, but I was determined to get my man. Finally, Bo pulled off leaving me in the open with no cover. The shooting continued. I see two more niggas shooting in my direction. I continued firing while backing up at the same time. I heard more shots. I would find out later that Keenan was also shooting with me. I turned and jogged towards Beatties Ford Rd. The place was in complete chaos as people was jumping into cars speeding away. I began looking for someone I could jump in the car with to get away. As I jogged, I heard a speeding car racing towards me I quickly spent around aiming my pistol. "Scoe get in" it was Bo, he came back for me. I quickly jumped in and we speeded towards Sylvania avenue to Bo's mom house. Bo ran inside to drop some money off in his stash. Bo used to go to his mom house and hide money. He did this for years. At the time of his death, Bo probably low-key had close to a hundred thousand put up. He was never flashy. When he came out the house, the argument started. "Man, why the fuck you left me in on the open like that nigga" "Nigga I told you to jump in, but you kept trying to be Rambo. I ain't got no gun on me. I said come on so we could get away but no, you trying to make a point" Bo said. "Man, f*** that I could have been killed" "Well we here now so it's all good." Me and Bo drove to the hood. It was about 1:30 in the morning. We were chilling in Beechway when one of the lil homies came running up to us. "Man, I was just robbed by some niggas in a blue Cadillac." He screamed. "Where at?" I asked." Man on Springview just now." We had heard that a blue Cadillac had been riding around the hood at night robbing people who was out. In fact, this Cadillac was on the news because they were robbing all over Charlotte. "Man, if I catch them niggas it's over." I spoke. About 45 minutes later we seen a blue Cadillac creeping down Springview Rd. That's them the lil homie said with excitement. The Cadillac stopped at the corner of Wellingford and Springview. It looked as if they were thinking if they should come down into the apartments for more victims. I started slowly walking towards them in the shadows. I didn't know if they see me

189

or not, but they had been sitting there for about three minutes. As I got closer, I could see that it was three people in the car. I stayed in the shadows. I stepped out the shadows and began walking very fast towards the car. The only thing I heard was " oh shit!!" Right before I raised my gun and fired into the car. The car speeded off as I continued to bust my gun. The car drove down Wellingford and turned onto North Tryon St. I ran back up the hill. Bo looked at me and said, "damn nigga you been in two shootouts in less than 2 hours". B- Zo looked at me. "For real!" He asked. "Man, Bo exaggerating" I said. I told Bo I would holla at him tomorrow. I gave everyone the KING handshake and walked towards my mother house. My mother was the one who always helped me to get away from the police. Whenever I was being chased, the neighbors would notify my mom's and tell her that they were chasing her son again. My mom would jump in her car and ride around until she seen me, and I would jump in the car. Once the police found out that she was helping me, they would always search her car whenever I was on the run. Everyone knew I never went to court. I always jump bail. It doesn't matter if it's a traffic ticket I ain't going to court. I never understood how people could just freely go to jail. I'm a runner. If you wish to put me into slavery you have to catch me first. I remember taking the police on a high speed chase through the hood. I was thirteen in a stolen car. The cops blue lighted me and I hit the gas. I was flying down Springview and made a sharp turn onto Kentbrook. Once I got to the top of Kentbrook I made another sharp turn onto Cinderella and headed towards Bilmark. Flying up Bilmark I rec the car turning on Snow White. There were at least three cars if police behind me. I jumped out and ran through someone yard and got away. I was always energetic and couldn't be still. I believe this was one of the main reasons I stayed in trouble. My parents couldn't afford to put me into programs or pay for summer camp etc. So, my fun consisted of getting into trouble. This is why now as a grown man I understand the youth that's constantly getting into trouble. I don't see them as trouble kids. I see them as poverty-stricken children with no hope because their parents can't afford the thing that society says you need in order to be someone great. These children just need guidance. Many do things to be accepted. I always thought that my so-called friends had just as much love for me as I did them but over the years while incarcerated, I started seeing the truth for what it was. They didn't have love for me personally. They love my courage and the work I put in for the hood. And many exploited my loyalty. But then I realized that I was the only one who kept doing long stretches while incarcerated. I asked myself many times " why am I the only who keeps going to jail?" I finally had to admit that my so-called friends had been telling on me since I was a kid. I never truly had a life because my life was dedicated to the hood, but the hood wasn't dedicated to me. But still I continued to love my hood. But deep down I knew that they really didn't fuck with me, they feared me. Where I loved them, they feared me. I would never bring harm to those I love but for some reason no one believed it. However, not one person who was my so-called friend can ever say I hurt them physically. My mom would always say: "Tray those are not your friends. They don't deserve your loyalty. I was taught loyalty at a very young age. My loyalty could never be bought because I never cared about money, so this made me a threat. However, many people misused my loyalty through manipulation. They knew how much I loved the hood, and some people would use that against me. Once I got older and realized this, I stopped trying to embrace everyone and started being a little distant. I felt that my path is a path I must travel alone, and that state was shown to be true after I was charged in the 2007 Hidden Valley Kings case. The next day I spoke with Keenan and he told me that he had my back the night before.

Him and Shug both were shooting at the guys who were shooting at me. I had no idea who the N*** was and it irk me. Keenan told me he would soon find out for me. I walked down to the block to see who was out, but it appears I'm the first. I started walking towards Hidden Valley apartments. As I was going into the African store, I ran into my partner lil Snake. Lil Snake was an Original King from Cedar Green. He was originally from the Derita and Mallard Creek area but hung in Cedar Green. We kicked it for a couple of seconds until we decided to link up. For a week straight, me and Lil Snake rode the streets of Charlotte terrorizing the city. This nigga had more enemies than me. In one week, we were in at least four different shootouts behind Snake. Snake had many people fearful of him in Charlotte. To be so small, Snake was an animal. He was a brown skin kid with low haircut and was skinny. He wasn't rapped too tight but was very smart. He took me to meet his kinfolk on polka white street. They had a very close family It appears that they were all neighbors on the same street. They even had a liquor house down in the cut at a dead-end street. We chilled and had a good time. Later me and Snake left and went to Cedar Green apartments. We were in a crack head car that Snake had. This car became the hottest car in Charlotte. I even told Snake that we had to ditch the car on more the one occasion, but he was hardheaded. While in Cedar Green we plotted our next move. Snake wanted to go to Dalton Village and rob the local hustlers that was trapping outside. I explained to him that we couldn't do that because I knew people over there and that every blue moon I still go there. So, we ended up going to Delahey Courts and robbing a few guys. Me and Snake argued every day and sometimes we even set trip. Like one day we got into it because I kept screaming out HVK. After a while Snake said " you must forget that this shit started in Cedar Green" I could tell he was irritated." I know where it started but yo hood dying off" I replied. " My hood ain't dead nigga" "Bullshit, where the fuck everybody at? We the only two walking through this motherfucker" I said while laughing. Snake wasn't laughing. In fact, we almost came to blows because he said I was set tripping. I was just speaking facts. However, Snake and our bond grew tight. We both had introduced our family to the other. Snake and I put in work daily. The work we put in I could never speak on, but I will say our work is documented in the hood history books.

Chapter 20

Roscoe

Just My Thoughts as I got older, I realized that many who claim or think that they're gangster are not. They are nothing more than a bunch of bullies. You see, a bully only picks and choose their battles. They attack those who they feel is less strong. They will never go at someone who they feel is more dominant. This makes them for what they really are, cowards. In the streets there are a few bullies. These guys like to show off in a crowd especially around women. They might see a guy who they know don't won't any problems and is not built in the way a real gangster is built. So, they go at these guys, putting on a show because they know there's no repercussions. But when a real gangster comes around, these street bullies get quiet, or they leave altogether. You see, real hitters don't have picks. They could care less if your body count was a hundred, you out of line, then someone is getting at you. Simple as that. However, throughout my years in the streets and being incarcerated, I've seen this type of behavior on many occasions. To me it's weak, it's lame and I never respected it. I respect those who stay in their own lane and not try to be what they're not.

The Hidden Valley Kings

We as New Afrikaans (blacks) especially us men, have to understand that Amerikkka has declared war on us. From the day our ancestors first touch this soil we have been attacked by white supremacy. All throughout slavery we were taught and trained to hate one another and ourselves. We were programmed to trust, love, respect, fear and serve our oppressor. They took away any and everything they thought would make us a man. We were stripped of our culture, God, religion, country, family, pride, and since we've been psychologically reprogrammed, we have been stripped of our minds. We have systematically been conditioned to hate ourselves. And through this hatred we have become our own worst enemy. We are still mentally slaves and must work continuously to come up out this cycle. FEDS I woke up early one morning headed to the block. I had to be careful because I had a warrant and had been on the run for a couple of months now. I was living with multiple girls at this time on Hoskins Rd. It was a three-bedroom apartment with eight people living in it. I was the only guy. Two of the girls were strippers and I loved them like my own. They were always there for me. They had boyfriends but their loyalty was to me. I try not to get involved in their love life but when they call, I come. I walked down the stairs and some of the women was up cooking breakfast. As I headed towards the kitchen, I seen a short dog Cadillac pull into the parking lot. I stopped to watch which apartment it was going to. I really couldn't see the driver because the windows were tented. "Roscoe you need to put something on your stomach" TT said. TT was from Cummings Ave. and was very pretty. She was about 16 years old and dated a guy from Greenville neighborhood. The guy was a well-known hustler in Charlotte and TT use to run over him. They had a baby together. There were a few times that TT use to hit his stash and bring it to me. I think he knew but never approached me about it. That would have been detrimental for him. As TT fixed my plate, I joked with a girl living with us while I sat at the table. Nicole grabbed my plate from TT and set int in front of me." Girl you know Roscoe don't eat pork" Nicole said to TT. "Bitch I know that. That's turkey." I ate my breakfast and called Boskee to come get me. We headed to the hood and over my mom's house. I had cut up a whole ounce that I got from Keenan and left it at my mom's. I ran inside and went to my stash. Something wasn't right. There appeared to only be about a thousand dollars' worth. When I left there was almost three thousand. I looked everywhere. "Ma, where's pops " I asked. She told me he left out early this morning and hadn't got back yet. I knew my father stole my shit. He always did.

But this time he took too much. I went outside and told Bo what happened. Bo shook his head. "Man, you know you can't leave that shit around Big Scoe" he said. We pulled off and went to Beechway. I knew where my father was. Every time he did some bullshit, he would run back to our old hood in Wilmore. I see one of the little homies and they told me they seen my dad on the city bus. I was upset. I asked if my dad mentioned where he was going and he said no. It wasn't until late that night my father came home. Me and Bo had just got back from the Gold Room and I asked him to stop at my mom's. It was about one in the morning. I went into the house and my father was sitting in the living room with a shot gun. "Son I know you mad, but I still got some left" he said. I looked at my father with anger in my eyes. He held up the bag. I snatched it out his hands. I looked into the bag. It looked to be over a thousand worth. I smiled and jumped back in the car. "Did he have it" Bo asked. "Yea" I said still smiling. " About fifty dubbs' missing I said. Back then we really only sold twenties. Dimes was more of a North Charlotte thing. Why are you smiling then" Bo asked thinking I lost my mind? " Because I thought I wasn't going see anything back". Me and Bo drove to Beechway apartments and posted up. We sat in the car taking turns on all the junkie sells. We stayed until about four in the morning and I had Bo drop me off on Hoskins Rd. I walked into the apartment and smelled nothing but weed, pussy and perfume. Only three of my homegirls was up. The four of us stayed up talking and plotting until the sun came up. Around 9:00am I still hadn't been sleeping and called a cab back to the hood. I was chilling on the block by myself when two carloads pulled up. Everyone had on a red bandana. When the first car stopped, I seen the passenger trying to quickly open his door. I immediately knew this wasn't good. I took off running as I was pulling my pistol out at the same time trying to find cover. I heard what sounded like a cannon and something went past my ear sounding like a bumblebee. I knew that sound all too well as I ran behind an empty parked school bus for cover. I only had a five shot 44. Bulldog revolver. I had about twenty more bullets in a plastic bag that I always kept with me. I finally made it behind the school bus and peeked around it. I see about three or four guys running jogging towards me. I shot back twice, and the guys stopped and began ducking and running for cover. I heard more shots. I could hear the bullets hitting the bus. I shot my last three bullets and quickly dumped the empty shells in my back pocket to flush down the toilet later. Just as fast as I unloaded, I reloaded. Bullets was still hitting the bus. I slapped the chamber back in place. "Fuck this shit" I said and came out from behind the bus and started shooting with so much accuracy that they started backing up. I took off running towards Beechway. As I ran towards the hill, I looked over my shoulder and seen one of the cars pulling in. This can't be happening I thought. As I made it to the top, I seen my man Keenan and I felt relieved. Without hesitation Keenan began firing two simi-automatic pistols at the car. The car went in reverse and by that time I had reloaded again and was shooting from behind the Beechway sign. As the car backed up, me and Keenan began walking side by side shooting at the car. Two cars of police pulled in to Beechway and me and Keenan took off running in the opposite direction. We ran past Keenan car that was parked in Seasorford apartments and cut through the path to Cinderella Rd towards Hidden Valley apartments. We got away. Hours later I found out that the shooting was a retaliation from something that happened that night. Apparently, some homies had kidnapped a well-known figure in Charlotte. They bound his hands and feet and drove to the Catawba River and threw him in. Somehow The binding wasn't tight enough and the guy was able to come up out of it and swim to the surface it was said that he made it back to his hood soaking wet. My homies didn't bother to tell no one else about it because they assumed, he was dead and that it really didn't much matter after that. But the n***** survive and I was caught off guard not knowing what was going on and was in a shootout behind my homies messy job. The next day I was chilling with Boskee. We were sitting in his car on the corner of Wellingford and North Tryon Street in front of the African store. We were listening to the rap group UGK and smoking weed when a cop car pulled up beside us. The cops new us all by name. "What's up Antwan" the cop asked. I tried to lean down in the seat so they wouldn't see me. But it didn't work. As soon as we locked eyes on each other both our car doors opened. Me running and the officer given chase. I ran towards Hidden Valley barber shop. The other cop that was on the passenger side gave chase with the car while the other officer ran on foot. I ran behind Hidden Valley barber shop which would take me through a path to Beechway apartments. I see Paco walking in my direction and tossed him the gun and kept running. The officer in the car drove behind the barbershop and hit me causing me to fall. As I stood up to run again the officer on foot tackled me back to the ground. I fought like hell but now it was two officers, and I was swinging like a mad. Finally, I was maced and hit in the head with something. I went down. As my eyes burned, I was cuffed and put in the police car. Ten minutes later an ambulance pulled up and I was put inside with officer and taken to the hospital. Once at the hospital I was cuffed to a bed and a doctor put these suctions like tubes on my eyeballs to flush out the mace. After about an hour I was transported to Central jail in downtown Charlotte. I was charged with failure to appear on an arm robbery charge. After processing I was sent to a pod for a few days until they sent me to the North Jail. I made all my necessary calls and I laid on my bunk to sleep. The next day I was chilling on the basketball court when a guy from Fairview Homes came in. I knew the guy and dated his sister all the way up until I was arrested. We talked for a while, and he told me he had 8 years for attempted murder. I told him he had to be more careful. My bond was 40,000 and I knew I probably had to sit for a minute. As the days went by, we began playing spades. My girl brother was always my partner. One day, he was talking trash to an older guy I knew. I knew this wasn't going to be good. The old head was locked in his cell. He yelled for the C.O. to pop his cell door. Soon as the door open the old head came out swinging. My man didn't stand a chance, so I grabbed the old head, he broke loose and was about to swing until he sees it was me. By that time my partner ran to grab a mop ranger but by that time the pod was flooded with C.O.'s. They locked them both up. I started chilling with some older guys who were on a fed case. I trusted these guys and we confided in one another. I didn't know much about how the FEDS work since I was only 18 and had never been in the federal system. I didn't know about 5k1's and Rule 35. But I would soon find out. One guy who I use to talk to did me dirty. I noticed he was going on attorney visit about three times a week. I didn't think anything of it. One day he came back from his visit and told me that the feds wanted me off the streets. I laughed it off. A couple days later I went for a bond hearing, and they refused to lower my bond. I was sent back to the pod and I knew I would be getting out that day. I played spades until my new was called and I was told to pack up because I made bail. I was driven to the Central jail to be released. But instead, I was 1099. 1099 is when you are already locked up, but they come with another charge while you are already in on another. They put a federal hold on me, and I couldn't make bond. I went through the process all over again. I was sent back to the North Jail as a federal inmate. They sent me back to my same pod. As soon as I went into the pod I asked where T was at and I was told he checked off. Checking off means you request to be moved to another pod because your life is in danger. I explained to everyone what happened, and an older guy pulled me to the side and told me to be careful who I spoke to while I was in the pod. He said niggas trying to go home and any information they can use they will. I was sentenced to 72 months for having a firearm by a convicted felon. I wanted to go to trial because they used my juvenile record to charge me as federal. The gun I was charged with was the gun that I used to rob the people in Countryside apartments. They really had no evidence since I was never caught with the gun and I also beat it in state trial. But everyone kept telling me that the feds had a 97.9 conviction rate. I decided to take the plea and go do my time. About a month after sentencing, I was put on the bus by the US Marshals and was driven to Atlanta holdover. The BOP has several holdovers. These holdovers are prisons that house federal inmates until they are classified. After classification you will designated to a particular prison. I was told that I'm going to Beckley FCI in West Virginia. While I was in Atlanta holdover, I met a few older guys from Charlotte. One guy, whose name was C.R. was my spades partner. At that time, we were allowed to smoke cigarettes in the feds. My mom sent me 50.00 so I could order commissary. One of the first things I ordered was a couple packs of New Ports. It wasn't long before a C.O. came to my cell door about 4:00 in the morning. "Abell, pack up." I jumped up and told the officer I was ready. An hour later I was cuffed along with about 40 other prisoners, and we all were led to the bus. I couldn't wait to get to the prison. This is my first time ever going to an adult prison and I couldn't wait. My young mind was too undeveloped to understand that this was a serious situation. As I got older and much wiser, I would be nervous because I understood the situations. I wasn't nervous out of fear. I was nervous because I'm walking into the unknown. But this thought process didn't hit until my mid-twenties. At that moment my mindset was "it is what it is". I arrived at FCI Beckley in 1998. We were escorted through the doors and was processed. I was told what unit I would be living in. I slowly walked towards my unit and was approached by a guy who asked where I was from. " Charlotte!!" I said with much force and base in my voice. There was only one other guy who was from Charlotte, but he acts as if he was trying to avoid me. We only had about two hours before lockdown, so I ran to the shower. My celly was a Vice Lord from Tennessee. That night he explained how the prison worked. He told me who was who. That morning we went to breakfast and my celly told me where the North Carolina homies sit at. I went to the table and sat down. Someone walked up behind me and said to me. " We can now finally kill your ass." I jumped up and turned around and was shocked at who I seen. END.

Acknowledgments

My mother Dorothy Miller, sister Nikki Abell McDonald my baby sister Rosie Abell my best friend Latasha Nesbitt, my father Roscoe Abell, my auntie Lily Gaston George Lester Jackson, Jonathan Peter Jackson Joka Khatari, Jeffrey Baldwin, all my niece's nephews, my book publisher Parice C. Parker and the new Afrikaans Revolutionary Nationalist.

FOUNTAIN OF LIFE PUBLISHER'S HOUSE

P. O. Box 92, LaGrange, GA 30241

Phone: 404.936.3989

For book orders or wholesale distribution

Website: www.pariceparker.biz

Thank You So Much!

www.pariceparker.biz

The Hidden Valley Kings

.

www.ingramcontent.com/pod-product-compliance
Lightning Source LLC
Chambersburg PA
CBHW070912270326
41927CB00011B/2536